Leaders of
Women's Suffrage

Other Books in the History Makers Series:

History MAKERS

Leaders of Women's Suffrage

By Kristina Dumbeck

Lucent Books
P.O. Box 289011, San Diego, CA 92198-9011

Library of Congress Cataloging-in-Publication Data

Dumbeck, Kristina
  Leaders of women's suffrage / by Kristina Dumbeck.
    p. cm.—(History makers)
Includes bibliographical references and index.
Summary: Profiles the lives and work of important American women
who fought for the female right to vote, including Elizabeth Cady
Stanton, Susan B. Anthony, Lucy Stone, Anna Howard Shaw, Alice
Paul, and Carrie Chapman Catt.
  ISBN 1-56006-367-X (alk. paper)
  1. Suffragists—United States—Biography—Juvenile literature.
2. Women—Suffrage—United States—History—Juvenile literature.
[1. Suffragists. 2. Women—Suffrage. 3. Women's rights. 4.
Women—Biography.] I. Title. II. Series.
  JK1898 .D85 2001
  324.6'3'092273—dc21

                                        00-008648

*On cover: Susan B. Anthony (standing) and Elizabeth Cady Stanton
(center), Carrie C. Catt (bottom right), Lucy Stone (bottom left), Dr.
Anna Shaw (top left).*

Printed in the U.S.A.

CONTENTS

The literary form most often referred to as "multiple biography" was perfected in the first century A.D. by Plutarch, a perceptive and talented moralist and historian who hailed from the small town of Chaeronea in central Greece. His most famous work, *Parallel Lives*, consists of a long series of biographies of noteworthy ancient Greek and Roman statesmen and military leaders. Frequently, Plutarch compares a famous Greek to a famous Roman, pointing out similarities in personality and achievements. These expertly constructed and very readable tracts provided later historians and others, including playwrights like Shakespeare, with priceless information about prominent ancient personages and also inspired new generations of writers to tackle the multiple biography genre.

The Lucent History Makers series proudly carries on the venerable tradition handed down from Plutarch. Each volume in the series consists of a set of five to eight biographies of important and influential historical figures who were linked together by a common factor. In *Rulers of Ancient Rome*, for example, all the figures were generals, consuls, or emperors of either the Roman Republic or Empire; while the subjects of *Fighters Against American Slavery*, though they lived in different places and times, all shared the same goal, namely the eradication of human servitude. Mindful that politicians and military leaders are not (and never have been) the only people who shape the course of history, the editors of the series have also included representatives from a wide range of endeavors, including scientists, artists, writers, philosophers, religious leaders, and sports figures.

Each book is intended to give a range of figures—some well known, others less known; some who made a great impact on history, others who made only a small impact. For instance, by making Columbus's initial voyage possible, Spain's Queen Isabella I, featured in *Women Leaders of Nations*, helped to open up the New World to exploration and exploitation by the European powers. Unarguably, therefore, she made a major contribution to a series of events that had momentous consequences for the entire world. By contrast, Catherine II, the eighteenth-century Russian queen, and Golda Meir, the modern Israeli prime minister, did not play roles of global impact; however, their policies and actions significantly influenced the historical development of both their own countries and their regional neighbors. Regardless of their relative importance in the greater historical scheme, all of the figures chronicled in the History Makers series made contributions to posterity; and their public achievements, as well as what is known about their private lives, are presented and evaluated in light of the most recent scholarship.

In addition, each volume in the series is documented and substantiated by a wide array of primary and secondary source quotations. The primary source quotes enliven the text by presenting eyewitness views of the times and culture in which each history maker lived; while the secondary source quotes, taken from the works of respected modern scholars, offer expert elaboration and/ or critical commentary. Each quote is footnoted, demonstrating to the reader exactly where biographers find their information. The footnotes also provide the reader with the means of conducting additional research. Finally, to further guide and illuminate readers, each volume in the series features photographs, two bibliographies, and a comprehensive index.

The History Makers series provides both students engaged in research and more casual readers with informative, enlightening, and entertaining overviews of individuals from a variety of circumstances, professions, and backgrounds. No doubt all of them, whether loved or hated, benevolent or cruel, constructive or destructive, will remain endlessly fascinating to each new generation seeking to identify the forces that shaped their world.

Seventy-Two Years of Struggle

In the United States before 1920, women did not have the right to vote in public elections. In most cases, they weren't even allowed to vote in church or school meetings and had practically no say in any of the laws governing their society. Their only means to participate in government was through their husbands and fathers. Many men and women believed that this was proper and natural. They reasoned that women were not equipped with adequate intelligence to make sound decisions about politics. A few enlightened women knew that this wasn't true. Those few dedicated their lives to changing society. They demanded woman suffrage—the right to vote—and although it took more than seventy years, eventually their demand was granted.

Today, women and men of all ages have these pioneers of the women's rights movement to thank for many of the privileges our society offers. Women who vote in elections, own property, have custody of their children, and hold public office owe them thanks. Husbands whose wives share the responsibility of earning the family income owe them thanks. And fathers who can proudly encourage their daughters to attend college and pursue the careers of their dreams also owe these remarkable women thanks.

Although thousands of women throughout the country worked diligently for woman suffrage, the women in this book represent a few of the truly extraordinary. These are women who committed nearly their entire lives to fighting for women's rights. They sacrificed their time, their money, and often their own happiness to make their nation a place that respected women. The six women in this book became more than just crusaders for women's rights; their work made them into American icons. Generations later, we recognize and appreciate their accomplishments.

During seventy-two years of struggle, these women organized a large movement and worked tirelessly to influence government at both the state and federal levels to change the laws and allow women to vote. Elizabeth Cady Stanton spearheaded the women's rights cause by calling the first women's rights convention in Seneca Falls, New York. Soon after, Susan B. Anthony joined Stanton and become a passionate leader and mentor to scores of women fighting for woman suffrage. Lucy Stone and her husband, Henry Blackwell, rallied to the cause and created the *Woman's Journal*, a suffrage publication whose influence reached thousands of American readers.

As the years passed, the National American Woman Suffrage Association (NAWSA), which became the largest organization of woman suffragists in America, was led by many

Members of the League of Women Voters demonstrate in 1970 to encourage women to vote.

strong, intelligent women. Among them was Anna Howard Shaw, a Methodist minister and medical doctor. Carrie Chapman Catt, known for her keen organizational skills and the "Winning Plan" that finally achieved suffrage, also served as NAWSA president for many years. Alice Paul, who led a militant suffrage organization, also played an important role in the suffrage effort.

The six women in this book fought a long and arduous battle, filled with disappointment, opposition, and challenge. But thanks to them and the thousands of people they led and inspired, ours is a country that offers liberty and justice for all—men and women alike.

CHAPTER 1

Votes for Women

In America during the nineteenth century, the right to vote and partic-ipate in democratic decision making was reserved exclusively for men. It was commonly thought that women should be concerned only with governing their households and raising their children. Furthermore, the female sex was seen as highly emotional and therefore lacking the dispassionate good judgment necessary to participate in government and politics. Because women had no say in the government of the so-ciety in which they lived, they had to rely on their husbands, fathers, or brothers to manage and protect virtually every interest.

But in the early part of the century, in spite of society's belief that women should not be concerned with government and social issues, women were becoming increasingly involved in many popular social reform movements. They were concerned with abolishing slavery, controlling drunkenness, and creating better educational opportuni-ties for women. Many women became active participants in social organizations to advance their causes. Their role, however, was still

Women first began to publicly promote the idea of suffrage for women in the nineteenth century.

considered inferior to that of the men involved. Women were typically given administrative and secretarial tasks such as fund-raising, tallying votes, collecting tickets at lectures, and taking minutes at meetings. They were never allowed to speak publicly, sit on committees, or vote on significant issues. Only men were accorded those important duties.

Women were also denied legal rights such as the right to own property. Any money or material possessions that a woman earned or inherited were considered the property of her husband. This even applied to the income earned by those women who took on extra work from outside the home—such as sewing or laundry—to help support their families. In addition, women had no legal right to divorce their husbands, although husbands were free to divorce their wives. And because women had no rights to property, if a husband decided to divorce his wife, he could not only leave her to bear the burden of raising their children alone, but he could take with him everything they owned, including land or possessions that his wife had inherited from her family.

Eventually, however, this social climate would lead women to realize the absolute need to gain the right to vote in order to secure the basic rights of free citizens, regardless of sex. This awareness eventually inspired a handful of brave women to band together and organize a women's rights movement.

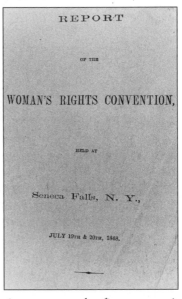

A report on the first women's rights meeting held in Seneca Falls, New York, in 1848.

The Origins of the Suffrage Movement

Women's struggle for the right to vote became known as the woman suffrage movement. During the nineteenth century, woman suffrage was becoming an issue in countries throughout the world. In the United States, the movement began in 1848 when two women, Elizabeth Cady Stanton and Lucretia Mott, organized the first women's rights meeting in Seneca Falls, New York. At this convention, they drew up the first public protest in America against women's political, economic, and social inferiority to men.

A procession of women to a brandy shop was meant to call attention to the abuses of women at the hands of their drunken husbands.

Most of the women who attended the meeting to begin the fight for women's rights had been active in other important social movements, namely abolitionism (the antislavery movement) and temperance (the antialcohol movement). Women involved in these social causes were demonstrating their desire to participate in social decision making and the government of their country.

The temperance movement strongly advocated the elimination of the consumption of alcohol. Temperance advocates, most of whom were women, saw alcohol as a source of some of the greatest problems of working-class wives and mothers. This class of women often suffered abuses at the hands of drunken husbands who would squander the family earnings on alcohol and often, in a drunken stupor, beat their wives and children. Women hoped that the temperance cause would reform this abusive and irresponsible behavior.

Abolitionism was an issue that attracted many influential men and women. Both Stanton and Mott, who would eventually devote a great deal of their lives to the struggle for woman suffrage, were enthusiastic abolitionists, as were their husbands. They were all closely associated with great abolitionist leaders like Frederick Douglass and William Lloyd Garrison. Indeed, Stanton and Mott met for the first time in London at an antislavery convention.

There, they shared their frustration at not being able to speak or participate in the voting within the organization because they were women.

It was years after their initial meeting in London, however, that Stanton and Mott met again and organized the women's rights meeting that became known as the Seneca Falls Convention. This history-making convention attracted many women abolitionists and temperance supporters who felt that if they had greater legal rights, they could do more to support their causes. At the convention, Stanton, Mott, and others were given a forum for their ideas about how to gain greater rights for women. One of the most significant things to come out of the convention was an important document known as the Declaration of Sentiments. The declaration, drafted by Stanton and based on the language and logic of the Declaration of Independence, proposed many reforms in favor of women's rights. These proposed reforms included a demand for a woman's right to vote, a demand so radical that many of the women who attended the convention, including Mott, feared it would actually damage the cause. However, Frederick Douglass, a respected former slave and leading abolitionist, supported Stanton's position. With his influence, the women at the convention voted to accept the declaration, suffrage demand and all. The Declaration of Sentiments stated, in part:

> Now, in view of this entire disenfranchisement of one-half of the people of this country, their social and religious degradation, in view of the unjust laws above mentioned, and because women do feel themselves aggrieved, oppressed, and fraudulently deprived of their most sacred rights, we insist that they have immediate admission to all the rights and privileges which belong to them as citizens of these United States.[1]

In addition to citing women's lack of the right to vote, the declaration also called for rectifying their lack of rights to divorce, to own property, and to acquire wealth. With this document, a determined movement for women's rights was born, with its first objective being the right to vote.

Arguments from the Opposition

Those who argued against woman suffrage—the "antis," as they were known by suffrage supporters—considered a woman's role to be determined by her sex alone, rather than by her individual capabilities or wishes. They cited Scripture that supported the idea of woman as "tender of the household." They also offered biological arguments, saying that women relied on "intuition and emotion" instead of "logic and reason," which would make females unsuitable for the concerns of government. The following sentiment, taken from a speech delivered at an antisuffragist meeting, sums up the ideas of many of the antis:

A woman's brain evolves emotion rather than intellect; and whilst this feature fits her admirably as a creature burdened with the preservation and happiness of the human species, it painfully disqualifies her for the sterner duties to be performed by the intellectual faculties. The best wife and mother and sister would make the worst legislator, judge, and police.[2]

An 1879 political cartoon sarcastically depicts an inauguration of a woman as president of the United States.

In addition, women were thought to be too delicate for political life. Women, the antis said, were weak and fragile, prone to fainting and mood swings. Just getting to the polls to vote would be dangerous and exhausting for the frail female. The antis also asserted that politics was a dirty business and respectable women would be corrupted by the harsh realities of the political arena.

Originally, suffragists based their defenses against the antis' arguments on the fact that if all men were created equal and had inalienable rights to political liberty, as stated in the Declaration of Independence, then women had rights to the same liberty. These early suffragists stressed the ways in which men and women were equal and alike, diminishing the differences between the sexes. Eventually, suffragists changed their argument. They reasoned that while they were still equal to men as individuals and citizens, they were different from men in many complementary ways. Their feminine perspective, many women felt, would bring balance and more accurate representation to government. Historian Alan Brinkley describes the revised suffragist position:

Suffrage . . . would not challenge the "separate sphere" in which women resided. It would allow women to bring their special and distinct virtues more widely to bear on society's problems. It was, they claimed, precisely because women occupied a distinct sphere—because as mothers and wives and homemakers they had special experiences and special sensitivities to bring to public life—that woman suffrage could make such an important contribution to politics.[3]

Suffragists used this kind of logic to disarm the opposition. Out of this contest grew a campaign to educate men and women across the nation on the value women could bring to government.

The Constitution: The Suffrage Battle After the Civil War

During the Civil War, the women's rights movement was temporarily suspended, putting the suffrage battle on hold. As most women's rights supporters were also abolitionists who felt strongly about the controversy between the northern and southern states, they threw themselves into the war effort, making notable contributions.

When fathers and sons were called to battle, wives and daughters took on the duties left behind. In some areas, women became solely responsible for farming as well as keeping up their usual household chores. In the cities, women became responsible for keeping family businesses going or took on jobs outside the home in order to meet their families' financial needs.

Women also supported war efforts by forming and joining groups to collect and produce first aid supplies and administer medical care to wounded soldiers. Before the war, nursing was considered a menial task—one that few women could be proud of as a serious profession. After the war, however, thanks to brave and determined women like Clara Barton, founder of the Red

Clara Barton, founder of the American Red Cross.

Fortieth Congress of the United States of America;

At the Third Session.

Begun and held at the city of Washington, on Monday, the seventh day of December, one thousand eight hundred and sixty-eight.

A RESOLUTION

Proposing an amendment to the Constitution of the United States.

Resolved by the Senate and House of Representatives of the United States of America in Congress assembled, (two-thirds of both Houses concurring) That the following article be proposed to the legislatures of the several States as an amendment to the Constitution of the United States, which, when ratified by three-fourths of said legislatures shall be valid as part of the Constitution, namely:

Article XV.

Section 1. The right of citizens of the United States to vote shall not be denied or abridged by the United States or by any State on account of race, color, or previous condition of servitude —

Section 2. The Congress shall have power to enforce this article by appropriate legislation —

Schuyler C. Fax
Speaker of the House of Representatives.

B. F. Wade,
President of the Senate pro tempore.

Attest:
Edward McPherson
Clerk of House of Representatives.

Geo. C. Gorham
Secy of Senate U.S.

The Fifteenth Amendment gave black men the right to vote and caused a split in the women's suffrage movement.

Cross, nursing became a trained and paid occupation that attracted many career-minded women.

In 1865, when the war ended, the right to vote became the main concern of women's rights supporters. Because the Constitution was being dramatically amended to abolish slavery, suffragists believed that this was their chance to gain voting rights for women. They expected that legislation giving blacks full citizenship would naturally do the same for women. In 1865, the Thirteenth Amendment was passed, abolishing slavery. But when the Fourteenth Amendment was passed in 1868, giving black men full U.S. citizenship rights, it contained language that specifically excluded women.

This exclusion caused a great stir among women's rights supporters. Now that black men had full citizenship rights, the next step proposed by the abolitionists would be to support passage of the Fifteenth Amendment, introduced in 1870, which gave black men the right to vote. The suffragists had to decide whether to keep fighting for both black men's and women's suffrage, or to separate altogether from those who supported black suffrage and work solely for women's right to vote. Because there were adamant suffragists on both sides of the issue, it would lead to a split in the young suffrage movement.

Dissension Among Suffragists

By 1869, suffragists had divided into two factions forming separate woman suffrage organizations, each with different positions on the Fourteenth and Fifteenth Amendments, as well as different ideas on how to advance the ideas of woman suffrage. One faction felt that the passage of the Fourteenth Amendment was a victory because it recognized black men as American citizens. This group also supported passage of the Fifteenth Amendment, believing it would eventually lead to women being granted suffrage as well. On the other side were those who felt that the Fourteenth and Fifteenth Amendments represented no progress at all because both failed to give women the same rights as black men.

The latter group became the National Woman Suffrage Association (NWSA), headed by Elizabeth Cady Stanton and Susan B. Anthony. NWSA proposed a Sixteenth Amendment that would specifically allow women the right to vote. Based in New York, NWSA focused on securing voting rights through constitutional amendment rather than pursuing them through individual state governments. In addition, NWSA adopted a somewhat radical tone by promoting a wide variety of feminist reforms including better educational opportunities, less restrictive clothing, and ownership rights for women.

The other organization that resulted from the split was called the American Woman Suffrage Association (AWSA), led by Lucy Stone and her husband, Henry Blackwell. Among this group's strong supporters were abolitionists and women's rights supporters Mary Livermore, Julia Ward Howe, Henry Ward Beecher, and Thomas Wentworth Higginson. The AWSA endorsed the Fifteenth Amendment, arguing that if women could not enjoy the right to vote, at least black men should. Nonetheless, they continued to fight for woman suffrage by rallying support through state organizations and by promoting their ideas through their suffrage publication the *Woman's Journal*. The AWSA strove to make woman suffrage seem less radical and offensive to those opposed. They sought to make new feminist reforms seem consistent with traditional American values.

Suffrage in the West

In the late 1860s, in spite of the differences in the two suffrage organizations, woman suffrage began making headway in many of the western states. Politicians and voters in several western states granted voting rights to women and even went to battle in Congress for the right to do so.

In 1869, Wyoming, which was still a territory, allowed women the right to vote. In 1890, when Congress denied Wyoming's ap-

Women voting in Wyoming, which was refused statehood as long as it allowed women the right to cast their ballots.

plication for statehood as long as it allowed women to vote, Wyoming declared, "We will remain out of the Union a hundred years rather than come in without the women."[4]

Other states soon followed Wyoming's lead. In 1870, the Utah Territory enacted woman suffrage and maintained it with statehood in 1896. Both Colorado, in 1893, and Idaho, in 1896, pioneered woman suffrage as well. These four states were the only ones to adopt woman suffrage in the nineteenth century. Not until 1910 did another state, Washington, grant women the vote. California followed in 1911, along with Oregon, Kansas, and Arizona in 1912.

A New Era in the History of Woman's Suffrage

In 1890, at the urging of younger suffragists, the leaders of the two separate suffrage organizations put their differences aside and merged into one large organization. This new organization, the National American Woman Suffrage Association (NAWSA), elected Elizabeth Cady Stanton as president, Lucy Stone as head of the executive committee, and Susan B. Anthony as vice president.

The new organization's strategy was to continue to demand an amendment to the federal Constitution while building support at the state level. The goal was to influence enough states to adopt suffrage amendments so that Congress would approve a federal amendment that at least three-fourths of the states would vote to ratify.

The organization also took on a more conservative stance, which it hoped would win it favor with the general public. Its members strove to minimize attention on some of the more controversial feminist issues and focus exclusively on gaining voting rights. They also went to great lengths to avoid association with radical causes and tactics that might offend the public, such as picketing, hunger strikes, and criticizing the political party in power.

Challenges in the South

The new NAWSA strategy sought to build support in the South, a region that presented much challenging opposition. The association with antislavery made women's rights a distasteful issue to the largely conservative white population in power. These conservatives did not like the idea that black men were being given the same rights as white men. This threatened their idea that white men should have control over government and community.

Suffrage leaders tried a new tactic designed to appeal to the ideals of the southern conservatives. They argued that rather than being a threat to white supremacy, woman suffrage could help restore it.

They explained that giving the vote to women who had attained a certain level of education would eliminate black women, since most had no formal schooling. Thus, the number of white voters would increase and the South could gain white supremacy in politics without having to disenfranchise black men.

Carrie Chapman Catt, one of the later NAWSA presidents, accompanied Susan B. Anthony on speaking tours through the South to promote this new argument. NAWSA even held its 1895 convention in Atlanta, Georgia, in order to gain the attention of southerners. But despite all efforts, by 1903 southerners were still very much opposed to the suffrage movement. Indeed, the southern state of Tennessee would be the last of all the states to agree to suffrage for women.

Another Split in the Movement

In 1912 the small series of victories in the western states inspired and reenergized suffragists across the country. About this time, a young suffragist named Alice Paul, who had recently returned from graduate studies in England, created a new controversy within the movement. Paul had been heavily influenced by the bold and brazen tactics of the militant British suffragists who staged regular protests, marches, picketing tours, and open-air speeches. Paul had no patience with the slow, state-by-state strategy being employed by the NAWSA. She did everything she could to encourage the organization to give up the tedious state campaigns and work solely toward a constitutional amendment guaranteeing woman suffrage.

Although this strategy was not well received by many suffragists, NAWSA did renew its campaign to work for an amendment. However, the organization, eventually parted ways with Paul. Her militant strategies, which included picketing, hunger strikes, and strong criticism of the president, did not agree with NAWSA's own strategic policy. Paul's insistence that suffragists oppose the reigning political party until it adopt woman suffrage was in direct violation of NAWSA's long-standing policy of nonpartisanship. So, Paul and her followers formed their own organization, called the National Woman's Party (NWP), and continued to pursue a federal constitutional amendment, often using daring tactics that were specifically directed against President Woodrow Wilson and his administration.

The Final Chapter

In 1915, Carrie Chapman Catt was elected, for a second time, to the presidency of NAWSA. Catt realized that although state work was necessary, it was paramount that the fight for an amendment to the Constitution remain its top priority. With this in mind, Catt initiated the "Winning Plan," which aimed the campaign at those

Suffragists demonstrate in front of the White House in 1917 with a banner that reads, "Mr. President, how long must we wait for liberty?"

states that had not yet adopted woman suffrage but seemed likely to come around with more encouragement.

During World War I, suffragists, most of whom were staunchly pacifist, put aside their feelings and supported the war effort however they could. This action gave them a patriotic image and boosted the respectability of their cause in the minds of many influential politicians, including President Wilson himself. By 1918, Wilson was showing support for woman suffrage, eventually leading Congress to approve the Nineteenth Amendment—drafted by Elizabeth Cady Stanton and Susan B. Anthony—giving women the right to vote. It was submitted for state approval a year later.

By 1920, suffragists were disheartened to find that although they needed the support of only one more state, legislative sessions were being suspended until the November election. So, in a desperate attempt to continue the momentum, suffragists urged President Wilson to hold special sessions to consider the Nineteenth Amendment. Eventually, Wilson was able to pressure Tennessee to call a session.

And so it was that, in Nashville, Tennessee, during the summer of 1920, the final battle over woman suffrage was fought and won. On August 26, Tennessee cast its vote for ratification and the Nineteenth Amendment to the U.S. Constitution was officially adopted. Thus ended the battle that had consumed suffragists for seventy-two years. The women who brought the struggle to victory weren't even born when the struggle began; the women who had begun the struggle were not alive to see the victory.

CHAPTER 2

Elizabeth Cady Stanton (1815–1902): Torchbearer for Women

Elizabeth Cady Stanton was born on November 12, 1815, in Johnstown, New York. She was born into a world in which women could not enter the professions or run businesses, nor were they permitted to attend universities. Because of their gender, they were not allowed to vote in public elections or hold political office.

Young Elizabeth spent a great deal of time in the office of her father, Daniel Cady. A lawyer and congressman, he dealt with many women for whom the law offered no rights or protection. Elizabeth was moved by the dozens of women who came begging her father for legal help. They complained of husbands who drank away the family income or who sold off their wives' inheritances. Elizabeth listened in frustration as her father explained to each woman that he could do nothing to help. The law did not permit women to own property, so legally a husband could do anything he wanted with the family home and money.

One day, Flora Campbell, a dear family friend who often stopped by with butter, eggs, cider, and other treats, came to Daniel Cady's office asking for help like so many women before her. Elizabeth, who loved Flora deeply, stood by her side as she tearfully explained her situation. Without her consent, her husband had mortgaged the valuable property that she had inherited from her father. Once again, Elizabeth's father could do nothing to help. He reached for his law books and read to Flora from them. Elizabeth, only ten years old, followed Flora out of the office and hugged her, exclaiming, "Dear Flora, don't cry another tear. I have all those wicked laws marked and I will cut every one out of the books tonight."[5]

Later, Flora returned in secret and told Cady what Elizabeth was planning. That night after supper, he took Elizabeth to his office and as they sat by the fire, he explained how laws were made. He told her that even if his law library burned down, it would not change things for women. Cady advised his daughter that when she grew up, she should go before the legislature and tell them everything she had seen and heard in his office. If she could persuade them to pass new laws, the old ones would disappear.

When Elizabeth was eleven, her only brother, Eleazer, died. He had just graduated from college with honors and his opportunities for the future had seemed limitless. Elizabeth's father was devastated. He sat in the dark parlor beside Eleazer's casket, bent over in grief. Elizabeth stole into the parlor hoping to comfort her father. The two sat silently until Elizabeth's father finally uttered, "Oh, my daughter, I wish you were a boy!"[6] And at that exclamation, Elizabeth firmly resolved to be the boy that he longed for. She joined a class of boys at school who studied Greek, Latin, and mathematics —unheard-of subjects for girls in those days. For three years, although she was the class's only girl and younger than most of the boys, she ranked second from the top. Nonetheless, upon graduation, she was not allowed to go to Union College where the boys went. Elizabeth was learning the limitations of her sex. She was also awakening to the battle for women's rights that lay before her.

Elizabeth Cady Stanton with one of her children.

Organizer of the Women's Rights Movement

In 1840, through her cousin, Gerrit Smith, a well-known antislavery activist, Elizabeth met Henry Stanton, an abolitionist and renowned lecturer. After only a few months of courting, they announced their engagement and were married later that year. A few days after their wedding they sailed for London to attend the World Antislavery Convention.

Elizabeth Stanton could see the need for women's rights within the antislavery organization. As she spent time with Lucretia Mott and other female abolitionists attending the convention, she became more and more aware of the limitations imposed on them. Women were not allowed to vote or participate in any decision-making procedures.

Stanton met Lucretia Mott (pictured), at an abolitionist convention.

They were expected to be satisfied to attend simply as observers, as women usually weren't even allowed to be present at business meetings.

The first convention meeting began with a plea by Wendell Phillips, a well-respected abolitionist and eventual women's rights supporter, for women to be made official members of the antislavery organization. The stormy debate that followed went on for hours, eventually ending in the defeat of Phillips's proposal. Stanton left feeling more impassioned about women's rights than ever before. She could not understand how these men could fight so strongly against the enslavement of blacks but do nothing about the similar bondage under which women chafed. Walking home that evening, Stanton and Mott discussed forming a women's rights association. They decided that they would hold a women's rights convention when they got back to America. Eight years passed, however, before this idea became a reality.

On her return from Europe, Stanton's main interest shifted from abolition to women's rights, which she continued to discuss in letters to Lucretia. In one passionate letter she wrote: "The more I think on the present condition of woman, the more I am oppressed with the reality of her degradation. The laws of our country, how unjust they are! Our customs, how vicious!"[7]

In the winter of 1842, the Stantons settled in Boston, where Henry was establishing a law practice. They were quickly introduced to an active and stimulating life of politics and law. Stanton made many new friends, both men and women, who shared her passion for women's rights.

Three years later, the Stantons moved to Seneca Falls, New York. Shortly afterward, Lucretia Mott, who was visiting a nearby town, invited Stanton to meet with her. Mott introduced Stanton to several other women who shared an interest in women's rights.

When Stanton proposed the idea of a women's rights convention, the women were all in hearty agreement. They planned the convention for the following week in Seneca Falls and immediately placed an ad in the Seneca County Courier. It read:

Woman's Rights Convention

A Convention to discuss the social, civil, and religious condition and rights of women will be held in the Wesleyan Chapel, at Seneca Falls, New York, on Wednesday and Thursday, the 19th and 20th of July current; commencing at 10 o'clock A.M. During the first day the meeting will be exclusively for women, who are earnestly invited to attend. The public generally are invited to be present on the second day, when Lucretia Mott, of Philadelphia and other ladies and gentlemen, will address the convention.[8]

The Declaration of Sentiments

Because a convention held by women was unprecedented, the planners decided to give it a sense of dignity and professionalism by asking Lucretia Mott's husband, James, to preside. They also decided to draft an official declaration, which they called the Declaration of Sentiments, that would express their ideas eloquently and memorably. Stanton suggested they use the Declaration of Independence as a model.

Abolitionist Wendell Phillips, proposed that women be made official members of the antislavery organization.

After they discussed the various points that declaration would cover, Stanton went home to enlist Henry's help in composing the document. The final version, thanks to Elizabeth's gift for writing and Henry's legal knowledge, became an eloquent demand for the equal treatment of women under the law. Henry also helped Stanton write a speech that she intended to deliver at the convention, as well as coaching her on how to gesture, enunciate, stand, and deliver the speech with confidence and professional skill.

Stanton also wrote the resolutions that constituted the women's official demand. Although she and Mott had already agreed on these resolutions, Stanton took the liberty of adding one more of her own—one that she had not discussed with Lucretia, one that even shocked her supportive husband. She included the demand for a woman's right to vote. Henry begged her to leave it out. He felt sure that such a radical demand would bring only misfortune. But Stanton maintained that if women had voting rights they could achieve their own reforms, without the help of men. When she showed the resolutions to Mott, just before the first meeting, Mott agreed with Henry.

Disappointed and yet determined, Elizabeth patiently listened as the convention meetings unfolded. When the Declaration of Sentiments was offered, almost everyone in the audience, men and women alike, added their signatures to it. As the resolutions were proposed and discussed, the audience voted in support of each one. Finally, it was Stanton's turn to speak. The audience received her warmly, and she rose, flushed and excited, to deliver her resolution that women be given the right to vote. She spoke with total conviction and eloquence. But when she finished, most people sat silently, stunned by this radical proposal. Only when the highly respected abolitionist Frederick Douglass stood up to back the resolution did the audience begin to show signs of support. When the matter was finally put to vote, it won by a small majority.

Abolitionist Frederick Douglass, backed Stanton's resolution that women be given the right to vote.

The press made a joke of the Seneca Falls Convention, calling it "the most shocking and unnatural incident ever recorded in the history of womaninity."[9] Before long, the fledgling women's rights cause was gaining so much negative attention that many women who had signed the declaration withdrew their names. Even worse, Stanton, now known as the mastermind behind the women's rights movement, was ridiculed and scorned everywhere she went. People even walked to the other side of the street to avoid her. But she kept on, organizing a new convention, this one to be held in Rochester, New York. Soon conventions followed in Ohio, Indiana, Massachusetts, Pennsylvania, and New York City. In spite of the eruption of anger and mockery that the Seneca Falls Convention had aroused, women's rights was a cause for which women around the country were beginning to fight.

Sun Flower

After the conventions, Stanton kept busy writing for local newspapers, answering the bitter attacks that were leveled against anyone who had participated in the now infamous women's rights conventions. She also agreed to many speaking engage-

Stanton befriended Amelia Bloomer, deputy postmaster in Seneca Falls.

ments, finding that she could earn money while educating the public about women's rights. Even in the face of opposition, Stanton enjoyed her new role as women's rights leader.

In the weeks that followed the conventions, Stanton befriended Amelia Bloomer, a woman who was serving as deputy postmaster in Seneca Falls. It was considered improper for a woman to hold this type of position, but Bloomer was determined to prove that if a woman had the skills and desire, she could perform any occupation she wished.

In addition to her work as deputy postmaster, Bloomer published a monthly paper called the *Lily* for her woman's temperance society. As her friendship with Bloomer grew, Stanton began writing articles regularly for the *Lily* under the pseudonym Sun Flower. Although the paper's primary purpose was to advocate temperance, Bloomer allowed Stanton to address ideas about women's rights in her articles.

Stanton had always been a gifted writer and soon had a dedicated following who eagerly scanned the paper for Sun Flower's startling, amusing, and stimulating articles. Eventually, Stanton

After the Civil War, Stanton (left) and Anthony resumed the fight for woman suffrage.

grew bolder, dropped the pseudonym, and began using her own initials. As E. C. S., she covered increasingly controversial subjects. She proposed an especially radical idea in her article entitled "Sewing." At that time, sewing was a task unquestioningly expected of women. Stanton criticized this view, writing that sewing was "a continued drain on sight and strength, on health and life, and it should be the study of every woman to do as little of it as possible."[10]

To many, her ideas about women's rights were shocking and disgraceful. But to some, her words were inspirational and encouraging. Stanton had launched a lifelong campaign against the empty traditions and misconceptions that kept women in bondage, and thanks to Amelia Bloomer's publication the *Lily*, the word was getting out.

A Lifelong Partnership

In 1851, Stanton met her lifelong friend and partner, Susan Brownwell Anthony. In May of that year, Anthony came to Seneca Falls to visit Bloomer, whom she knew through her temperance work. Bloomer introduced Anthony to Stanton, and later, they all sat down at Stanton's home for a spirited conversation about abolition, temperance, and women's rights. By the time Anthony's visit ended, Stanton knew that she had a staunch ally.

From then on, the two corresponded and collaborated whenever they could. Their shared interests in temperance and antislavery provided them many opportunities to meet and compare ideas. Anthony turned to Stanton for advice on public speaking, strategy, and writing as she diligently worked for the temperance cause. To Stanton, however, temperance was secondary to women's rights. Stanton believed that women could not make serious strides for temperance until they had greater legal rights, including the right to vote.

As her family grew, Stanton felt more and more suffocated by the domestic duties that kept her away from her career in women's rights. Only at night, when the day's chores were done and the children were tucked in their beds, could she steal a few hours to write a speech or tract for the cause. As Anthony became a dedicated women's rights supporter, she spent more time with Stanton, helping her with household errands and caring for the children so that Stanton could write. Often Anthony had to inspire Stanton, who frequently felt that she couldn't do anything for women's rights until her children were grown.

Woman Suffrage Comes Last

As tensions mounted over slavery throughout the country, civil war appeared more and more inevitable. Stanton awaited the war anxiously, feeling that the sooner it got underway, the sooner slavery would be put to an end. Anthony did not share her feelings. Her Quaker upbringing, with its pacifist tenets, turned her against war for any reason. Instead of joining Stanton and others in supporting the war as a means to free the slaves, Anthony rallied against it and put all her energies into turning the public's attention to women's rights. But with war looming, no one was interested. Even Stanton encouraged Anthony to give the women's rights battle a rest and do what she could to educate women about the issues surrounding the war. Together, Anthony and Stanton brainstormed ideas to get women more involved in this critical period of their country's history.

In 1863 the two women decided to form the Women's National Loyal League to educate women on current matters of politics and social reform, especially those concerning the war. The group's first action was to circulate a petition demanding that Congress pass a constitutional amendment abolishing slavery. Anthony and Stanton traveled throughout the country, gathering signatures. By August 1864, four hundred thousand signatures had been obtained. A year later, the Thirteenth Amendment was passed at President Abraham Lincoln's recommendation. Slavery had finally been abolished, and women across the nation felt proud of their crucial part in achieving this victory.

But the battle was not over. Although slavery was no longer legal, black men still did not have full citizenship and they, like women, could not vote. Stanton and Anthony hoped that antislavery advocates and women's rights advocates would join forces, as they had in

Bust of Lucretia Mott, Elizabeth Cady Stanton, and Susan B. Anthony, stands in capital building, Washington, D.C.

the past, to achieve voting rights for both women and African Americans. But much to their disappointment, the Antislavery Society felt that linking woman suffrage with black suffrage would weaken the cause for blacks.

Woman suffrage advocates pointed out that during the war, women had demonstrated their ability to contribute to the nation's welfare. They argued that their war activities proved that they were worthy of full citizenship, including the right to vote. But the newspapers proclaimed it the "Negro's hour." To Stanton, there was a crucial flaw in this celebration of the black race's newfound freedom—it didn't include females. In a letter to Wendell Phillips, president of the Antislavery Association, she wrote:

> May I ask in reply to your fallacious letter just one question based on the apparent opposition in which you place the Negro and woman. My question is this: Do you believe the African race is composed entirely of males?[11]

The troubling differences arising between the two causes caused Stanton to regret that she had encouraged Anthony to give up the women's rights struggle during the war. Stanton now realized that their main objective should have always been women's rights. From now on, their loyalties would be to women first, and their primary goal to gain woman suffrage.

A Great Disappointment

It was difficult to ignite interest in woman suffrage while the country was still recovering from the war, but Stanton and Anthony were not daunted. They began circulating a new petition, which read:

> To the Senate and House of Representatives: The undersigned women of the United States, respectfully ask an amendment to the Constitution that shall prohibit the several states from disenfranchising any of their citizens on the grounds of sex.[12]

The petition made its way to Congress by the end of the 1865–66 congressional session and represented the first formal request made by women for congressional action on woman suffrage. The request was denied, but Stanton and Anthony didn't give up. When the Fourteenth Amendment guaranteeing black men citizenship was before Congress, they tried again from another angle, demanding that the word "male" be stricken from the amendment. Again, their request was denied.

Disagreements between the antislavery cause and the women's rights cause persisted. On July 28, 1868, the Fourteenth Amendment was officially added to the Constitution, ensuring that all male persons, black and white, had full citizenship under the law. This did not, however, guarantee black men the right to vote. It became apparent to antislavery supporters that a fifteenth amendment would be necessary. Stanton and Anthony were determined to see that the new amendment include voting rights for women as well. Once again, they circulated petitions. But the abolitionists refused to sign. They didn't want to support women until black men had achieved the right to vote.

Angered and frustrated, Anthony and Stanton decided to ask for a sixteenth amendment specifically granting woman suffrage. Through her political connections, Stanton managed to get the Sixteenth Amendment introduced during the next session of Congress. In 1869, Stanton and Anthony began a tour of western states to urge politicians to vote for the amendment. The successful first leg of their tour, however, left them totally unprepared for what they came home to. Arriving back in New York, they learned that many original supporters of the women's movement were beginning to side with abolitionists.

These differences of opinion could not be resolved. Eventually, two separate woman suffrage associations emerged from the conflict. Stanton and Anthony formed the National Woman Suffrage Association (NWSA), whose presidency Stanton held for the life of the organization. This group worked primarily for the passage of the Sixteenth Amendment—the Woman Suffrage Amendment. The group that sided with the abolitionists, headed by Lucy Stone and her husband, Henry Blackwell, formed the American Woman Suffrage Association (AWSA). Their plan was to work for both black and woman suffrage. For the next twenty-one years, the two associations would fight separately for woman suffrage.

Suffragists Around the World Unite

Since her honeymoon in Europe, Stanton had dreamed of uniting women around the world for the sake of women's rights. She and Anthony decided to bring a proposal before the NWSA for an international gathering of women. NWSA members agreed that holding such a gathering would be the perfect way to celebrate the fourth decade of the woman suffrage movement.

On Sunday, March 25, 1888, the conference, held in Washington, D.C., was kicked off with Stanton at the helm. The delegates who arrived from all over the world made up the largest assembly of women ever. The conference was a huge success, generating good press for women's rights and giving woman suffrage a showcase. Also, now that women were coming together internationally, the women in the two separate American suffrage associations began to talk about putting aside their differences and bringing together their resources. They had, after all, been working for years toward the same goal.

As the international conference came to a close, the American Woman Suffrage Association and the National Woman Suffrage Association agreed to begin to merge into a new organization called the National American Woman Suffrage Association (NAWSA). With Stanton as their president, the members agreed to pursue the goals of both former organizations: working state by state to gain support, as well as continuing to push Congress to pass the Sixteenth Amendment to the Constitution.

Stanton served as president of NAWSA for four years before turning her attention to other projects. At the 1892 NAWSA convention, at the age of seventy-seven, she announced her official retirement and asked that Anthony be elected president in her place. In her final speech, Stanton reminded the audience of the principles for which the women's movement had always stood:

> In discussing the rights of woman, we are to consider, first what belongs to her as an individual, in a world of her own, the arbiter of her own destiny. . . . Secondly, if we consider her as a citizen, as a member of a great nation, she must have the same rights as all other members, according to the fundamental principles of our Government. Thirdly, viewed as a woman, an equal factor in civilization, her rights and duties are still the same—individual happiness and development.[13]

Though Stanton officially retired from her NAWSA duties, she did not resign involvement in woman suffrage. She did all she could to support Anthony and NAWSA by writing dozens of speeches and articles. Just after her eightieth birthday, Stanton published volume 1 of *The Woman's Bible*, a book that she had been working on for several years. She intended it to make women question the discriminatory implications of biblical texts. In her memoirs, she wrote:

> Seeing that religious superstitions of women perpetuate their bondage more than all other adverse influences, I feel impelled to reiterate my demands for justice, liberty, and equality in the Church as well as in the State.[14]

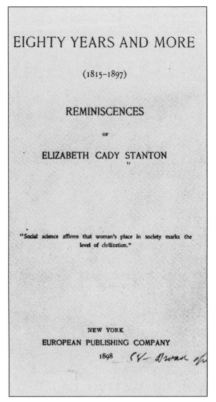

EIGHTY YEARS AND MORE

(1815–1897)

REMINISCENCES

OF

ELIZABETH CADY STANTON

"Social science affirms that woman's place in society marks the level of civilization."

NEW YORK
EUROPEAN PUBLISHING COMPANY
1898

Stanton wrote in her memoirs that religious superstitions perpetuated women's bondage.

The book sparked a gigantic controversy nationwide, proving that even in her last few years Stanton could impassion people.

On October 26, 1902, at the age of eighty-seven, Stanton died peacefully. Although she had worked fifty-four years in service of woman suffrage, she lived to see only four states give women the vote.

CHAPTER 3

Susan B. Anthony (1820–1906): "Failure Is Impossible"

Possibly no woman in history is more famous for her service to the women's rights cause than Susan Brownwell Anthony. She was born in Adams, Massachusetts, on February 15, 1820. Her father, Daniel Anthony, was a devoted member of the Quakers, well respected and loved in the Quaker community. The Quakers allowed all members, including women, to speak freely in the meetings that were frequently held to discuss church business. Growing up in a community that treated women as equal partners led Susan to believe that women everywhere were treated this way.

Susan B. Anthony grew up in a Quaker community where women were treated as equal members.

She found out otherwise when she was still a young girl. Smart and an excellent student in every school subject, especially mathematics, Susan was bitterly disappointed one day when her teacher told her that she would not be taught long division like the boys in her class. When she questioned this, her schoolmaster said that girls needed to know only enough arithmetic to "weigh butter and count eggs."[15] Even Susan's father, whom she loved and admired, failed her when he decided to send her to a seminary for girls instead of an academy where women could study all the subjects that men studied, including science and math.

When Susan was still a young woman, living at home with her family, she was invited by her uncle to head the girl's department of Canajoharie Academy. The offer was a dream come true. Not only did it allow her to become a professional teacher and earn her own money, but she was also contributing to the education of young girls, something she felt was extremely important to the future of women. And because her uncle was not a Quaker, Susan had the opportunity to live in an entirely different environment. For the first time in her life, she could attend the theater, the circus, parties, dances, and dinners. Susan also began to study the laws that controlled women. She soon decided to dedicate her life to improving the status of girls and women.

Anthony Meets Elizabeth Cady Stanton

In 1845, while still teaching at Canajoharie, Anthony heard about a women's rights convention to be held in Seneca Falls, New York. Because her teaching duties did not allow her to attend, she attentively followed the story of the convention through newspaper accounts. Although she strongly agreed with what Elizabeth Cady Stanton and Lucretia Mott said about better education for girls, equal pay, freedom for women to pursue careers of their choice, and women's rights to property and custody of their children, she was shocked and amused by their suggestion that women should have the right to vote. She was even more shocked to find, on returning home for a visit, that her entire family had attended all of the convention meetings and heartily supported Stanton's ideas about woman suffrage.

The Anthony family had moved to Rochester, New York, and their house had become a meeting place for antislavery activists, including the well-known former slave Frederick Douglass. The entire family were active supporters of temperance as well as abolition. Although Susan was away at school teaching, she too was a strong advocate of both causes, giving talks and attending meetings on the subjects whenever she could. After the Seneca Falls Convention, Susan's family convinced her that women should have the right to vote. But, already busy supporting temperance and abolition, she felt that she simply did not have time to devote herself to another cause.

Anthony changed her mind, however, as she realized that the lack of rights for women weakened her efforts to help the temperance and antislavery causes. This fact was brought home during a convention in which the Daughters of Temperance and the Sons of Temperance organizations met in Rochester. On the second day of the convention, Susan stood up to tell the audience what the Daughters of Temperance had accomplished for the cause. She was astonished when the chairman looked at her in horror and yelled, "The Daughters of Temperance were asked here not to speak, but to listen and learn!"[16] With that, Susan decided that she would have to fight for women's rights before she could make any progress for other causes.

As her interest in women's rights grew, Anthony became acquainted with other women who shared her passion. One night, after attending an antislavery meeting in Seneca Falls, New York, Anthony met her future lifelong friend and collaborator, Elizabeth Cady Stanton. Anthony and Stanton liked each other at once and soon joined forces to work for women's rights. Combining their talents—Stanton's for writing and Anthony's for oratory—they came up with ideas for temperance, antislavery, education, and women's rights lectures. As a team, they quickly gained popularity and received invitations to speak at conventions across the nation.

The First Woman's State Temperance Society

In 1853, Anthony returned to Rochester to work with the Daughters of Temperance, of which she was then president. She worked steadily, starting new women's clubs and campaigning for temper-

Anthony (right) combined her talent for oratory with Elizabeth Cady Stanton's speech writing ability to further the women's rights cause.

Anthony organized the first Woman's State Temperance Society in New York.

ance wherever she could. Much to Anthony's delight, the organizations and clubs she started grew successfully. Even the Sons of Temperance took notice of their success and invited Anthony to a convention in Syracuse.

Although this invitation appeared to be a gesture of cooperation, it was not. When Anthony arrived at the gathering, she was told that the organization objected to the presence of women at their meetings. She was asked to leave, even though she had been personally invited. Anthony took a seat anyway. Not surprisingly, this angered the men in the meetinghouse. The man at the platform shouted, "This meeting will not resume until the females are put out into the street!"[17] Anthony stood to tell the men about the accomplishments of the Daughters of Temperance, but her words were drowned out by the shouting men. Anthony continued with her address anyway, then left. On her way out, she made arrangements to hold a women's meeting that very night in a local church. The next night, she held another meeting. By the second day, she was receiving so much attention that people came to her meetings instead of those held by the Sons of Temperance. Soon after, Anthony organized the first Woman's State Temperance Society. Stanton was elected president and Anthony was secretary.

Now that they had their own organization, free of the limitations that had been placed on them by their male counterparts, the women took aggressive action. Their goal was to raise enough petitions to get the New York state legislature to pass a law prohibiting the use of liquor. Anthony quit her teaching job to write letters, raise money, and rent meeting halls where Stanton and others could speak against drunkenness. In spite of all their efforts, the legislature rejected Anthony and Stanton's petition because most of its twenty-eight thousand signatures were those of women and children. This would not be the last time Anthony's efforts would be thwarted because of her sex, but she now became completely convinced that women must have the same constitutional rights as men.

The Married Woman's Property Law

In 1853, Anthony began a difficult and vigorous campaign for women's property rights. By law, women were not allowed to own property, keep their own wages, have custody of their children, or sue their husbands for divorce. In trying to rally support for her other causes, Anthony realized that women couldn't help much if they weren't allowed to control their own money. She found that many of the groups she had organized had disbanded because the

Women's temperance groups were often forced to disband because they lacked funds.

women didn't have money to pay speakers or to subscribe to temperance and antislavery papers. In her diary Anthony wrote:

> Woman must have a purse [money] of her own, and how can this be, so long as the Wife is denied the right to her individual and joint earnings. Reflections like these, caused me to see and really feel that there was no true freedom for Woman without the possession of all her property rights, and that these rights could be obtained through legislation only.[18]

Anthony traveled throughout the state of New York, speaking at meetings, collecting signatures for petitions, and lobbying the legislature.

During her travels, Anthony stayed in taverns and boardinghouses because hotels generally refused to rent rooms to a woman unless she was accompanied by a man. In these places, Anthony saw women working themselves to the bone serving guests, caring for children, making up beds, and cleaning rooms. Yet, it was always their husbands who came around to collect the rent. Anthony used these observations in her speeches. She captivated her audience with stories of women whose property was taken away from them; women who were torn away from their children; women who worked day and night for wages they never saw. But although her audiences were usually fascinated, Anthony was at times disappointed by the paltry attendance. Women in those days rarely left their homes unaccompanied by men. At one meeting, Susan waited for quite some time before six men arrived to hear her speak. Later, after deciding she wasn't a "fanatic" as the newspapers had claimed, the men went home and returned with their wives.

Though Anthony spoke at any opportunity—in churches, at teachers conventions and antislavery and temperance meetings, and even in hotel lobbies and dining rooms—she found the most effective place to arouse enthusiasm for the cause was at women's rights conventions. Discussions at these conventions covered a broad range of issues. Anthony addressed the subjects of coeducation, freedom of speech, freedom of religion, equal pay and better employment opportunities, women in government, women's fashion, and the need for exercise and good hygiene, as well as property rights, divorce rights, and custody rights. With help from Stanton and others, she organized national gatherings at which women from as many states as possible would meet to discuss these ideas. Attendees would then take what they learned to their towns and cities and spread the word in a grass-roots movement.

As women in New York, as well as across the nation, became better educated about women's issues, Anthony and Stanton seized the opportunity to gather support for a women's property rights bill. In March 1860, Anthony and Stanton were invited to speak before the New York legislature on behalf of married women's property rights. The next day, the assembly passed the Married Women's Property Bill. The bill stated that a married woman could own property, real and personal, and could hold a job or perform any service on her own, keeping whatever she earned. Under this new law a woman could sue and be sued; she could buy, sell, and make contracts; and she was the joint guardian with her husband of their children. Anthony and Stanton had won their first big victory.

The Woman's National Loyal League

The onset of the Civil War presented new challenges for Anthony and other women's rights crusaders. Although most of them were dedicated antislavery supporters, they were fiercely against the war. Anthony was especially opposed because her Quaker upbringing had taught her that war for any reason was wrong. Nonetheless, she felt that she and other women should do what they could to help the government end the war quickly so that slavery would be abolished forever. In her diary she wrote:

> I wish the government would move quickly, proclaim freedom to every slave and call on every able-bodied Negro to enlist in the Union Army. . . . To forever blot out slavery is the only possible compensation for this merciless war.[19]

With the energies of the country consumed by war, the women's rights movement was all but forgotten. But Anthony thought the cause should be pursued. When she discussed organizing a women's rights convention with Stanton, Stanton discouraged it. She felt that the country needed their support. The time for women's rights would come later.

Once the war was underway, Anthony and Stanton discussed what they and other women could do to serve their country. Already women were responding to the crisis bravely. In many places, they not only worked their farms and ran the family businesses while their sons and husbands were away fighting, but many of them provided sewing, knitting, and nursing care for soldiers. Although Anthony was proud of the work women were doing, she felt that many of them lacked a necessary intellectual awareness of the central issues of the war. She believed that if women beter understood national politics, they would also be better voters when their time came.

Eventually, Anthony and Stanton, with the help of their friend and fellow suffragist Lucy Stone, organized the Women's National Loyal League, through which they sought to educate as many women as possible about the war, slavery, and politics in general. At their first meeting, Anthony and Stanton explained to the women attending that the war was being fought not only for the Union but to preserve the American way of life based on freedom and equal rights. They also circulated petitions asking for an act of Congress to emancipate any black person being held involuntarily. Anthony rented an office in New York from which she printed petitions to be mailed across the country. To each petition she attached the following message:

> There must be a law abolishing slavery. . . . Women, you cannot vote or fight for your country. Your only way to be a power in the government is through the exercise of this one, sacred, constitutional "right of petition," and we ask you to use it now to the utmost.[20]

In April 1864, the Thirteenth Amendment abolishing slavery passed the Senate, and Anthony was hopeful that before long it would be ratified and officially added to the Constitution.

The Susan B. Anthony Amendment

Once the war ended, differences grew between suffragists and abolitionists over the passage of the Fifteenth Amendment, which gave black men the right to vote. This amendment, which did not give women the right to vote, drew deep disappointment and resentment from those women who had been so dedicated to the antislavery cause.

Many women's rights supporters, including Anthony and Stanton, felt that women should disassociate themselves from the antislavery group and focus entirely on women's rights. But another group of supporters, led by Lucy Stone, felt that they should continue working with antislavery supporters to fight for the rights of both blacks and women. As a result, two factions of the women's rights movement were born. Anthony and Stanton led one, and Lucy Stone led the other.

Anthony's group became the National Woman Suffrage Association (NWSA), made up of women from nineteen states, with Stanton as president and Anthony as a member of the executive committee. The main objective of the NWSA was a sixteenth

A political cartoon depicts Anthony's desire to vote as threatening to men.

amendment—or Suffrage Amendment—to the Constitution. This proposed amendment read "The right of citizens of the United States to vote shall not be denied or abridged by the United States or by any state on account of sex." Although the Suffrage Amendment was not adopted until 1920, long after Anthony's death, it has become known as the Susan B. Anthony Amendment.

Anthony Casts a Ballot

As the 1872 presidential election approached, Anthony encouraged supporters of woman suffrage to take whatever measures necessary to draw attention to the issue. She reasoned that women already had the right to vote, according to the language of the Fourteenth Amendment, which stated, "No State shall make or enforce any law which shall abridge the privileges or immunities of citizens of the United States." So she urged women to exercise their rights by registering and voting in the election.

So convinced was Anthony that this action was necessary that two days before the election, she persuaded fifteen of her friends to join her in registering. Their action was mentioned in the evening paper, and soon more women followed their lead. Then, on November 5, 1872, the morning of the vote, Anthony and her three sisters, arm in arm, entered the polls to cast their votes. Before the officials realized what they were doing, nearly seventeen women had officially voted. That day, Anthony wrote to Stanton:

> Well, I have gone and done it!!—positively voted the Republican ticket—Strait—this A.M. at 7 o'clock—& swore my vote in at that. . . . All my three sisters voted—Rhoda deBarmo too—Amy Post was rejected & she will immediately bring action against the registrars. . . . Not a jeer not a word—not a look—disrespectful has met a single woman. . . . I hope the morning's telegrams will tell of many women all over the county trying to vote. . . . I hope you voted too.[21]

Anthony's trip to the polls won her immediate attention from the press across the country. Many favorable accounts claimed her act would go down in history. However, several papers mocked and condemned the act, calling it "female lawlessness" and saying that Anthony's disregard for the law had proved women unfit for the vote.

All was quiet for about two weeks. Anthony and the other women voters wondered if their action had been forgotten. But on November 18, a U.S. deputy marshal rang the doorbell and announced to Anthony that he had come to arrest her. As a gesture of protest, Anthony held out her hands for handcuffs. The embarrassed marshal, however, declined to use them. When they got to the streetcar and Anthony was asked for her fare, she announced that she was traveling at the expense of the government. Pointing to the marshal, she told the driver that he would have to pay her way.

A hearing was set for November 29, at which time Anthony and the others were fined $500 each. Anthony refused to pay. The jury was not allowed to deliberate over this punishment; instead, the judge ordered them to bring in a verdict of guilty. In the final ruling, Anthony was fined $100, which she never paid.

Anthony was tried for registering and voting illegally in the 1872 presidential election.

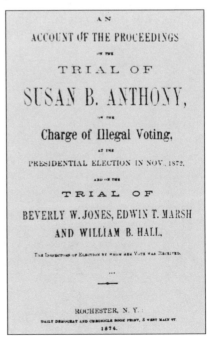

"Failure Is Impossible"

In 1890, after twenty-one years of operating as two separate organizations, the National and American associations combined to
form the National American Woman Suffrage Association
(NAWSA). The fact that Anthony never married or had family responsibilities to take her away from the cause allowed her to work
for many years as president of NAWSA. During her last year as
president, she focused on preparing the younger women in the association for the road ahead.

In the summer of 1899, Anthony traveled to London, where she
headed the U.S. delegation to the International Council of Women.
On returning home in August, Anthony immediately began to make
arrangements to turn over her NAWSA presidency to one of the
younger women. Although the new president would ultimately be
elected by a vote of the members, Anthony fully intended to use her
considerable influence to ensure the choice of Carrie Chapman
Catt, a promising young woman with a talent for organization and
a special gift for directing her followers and winning their trust and
dedication. She was also extremely good at raising money, a skill
that Anthony recognized would carry special importance in the
years of campaigning that lay before them.

*In 1899, Anthony (center) headed the U.S. delegation of the International
Council of Women.*

The main objective of the National American Woman Suffrage Association was the Suffrage Amendment, known as the Susan B. Anthony Amendment.

Anthony's last convention, in February 1900, was both sad and joyful. She presided over the meetings with a great sense of pride in the women whom she saw before her. As difficult as the official process must have been, she conducted herself with her trademark manner of grace and good cheer. She addressed the group with a mixture of motherly tenderness and professional dignity:

> I am not retiring now because I feel unable, mentally or physically, to do the necessary work, but because I wish to see the organization in the hands of those who are to have its management in the future. I want to see you all at work, while I am alive, so I can scold you if you do not do it well.[22]

After her retirement, Anthony continued to work diligently for women's rights, faithfully attending the NAWSA conventions every year and providing her successors with her highly sought-after advice and opinions. She also continued to support the International Council of Women, traveling to Berlin with her sister and several friends for the 1904 conference.

Anthony died at her home in Rochester on March 13, 1906. Asked a few years before her death if she believed that women would ever be given the vote, she replied, "It will come, but I shall not see it. . . . It is inevitable. We can no more deny forever the right of self-government to one-half our people than we could keep the Negro forever in bondage."[23] To her successors she left her legacy of the struggle for justice and her promise that "Failure is impossible." Although she spent nearly her entire life working to achieve woman suffrage, she was correct in her prediction that she would not live to see women earn the right to vote. Nonetheless, she left a torch burning for others to carry on.

CHAPTER 4

Lucy Stone (1818–1893): Voice of the Women

Lucy Stone, born on August 13, 1818, grew up on a farm just outside West Brookfield, Massachusetts. As a girl, she read the biblical passage "Thy desire shall be to thy husband, and he shall rule over thee." The young Lucy was horrified. She knew that most men, including her own father, held this view, but she had never imagined that it came from the Bible. Stunned, Lucy ran to her mother, who explained that the "curse of Eve" made it a woman's duty to submit to her husband. Lucy made up her mind that she would go to college and study Greek and Hebrew so she could read the Bible in its ancient forms. She refused to believe that the translation she had read could be correct.

When Lucy was twelve, her mother's health began to fail, a result of chronic overwork. Lucy helped by taking on many of her mother's chores. She rose early on Monday mornings to do the entire family's wash, hang it out to dry, walk a mile to school, and come back at noon to bring in the clothes. Then she would return to school. After school, she would perform her regular chores as well as help her mother with the cooking and cleaning. At night, when all the work was done and everyone was in bed, Lucy stayed awake to study.

Lucy thought it was wrong that her mother, like all women, had to work so hard, doing whatever their husbands said without question. She wondered

At an early age, Lucy Stone resolved to change women's servitude to their husbands.

why women didn't simply refuse to obey. As she got older, she realized that it would take years of work and a lifetime of dedication to change the situation. But that is exactly what she intended to do.

Oberlin Collegiate Institute

Although Stone's father did not support her desire to go to college, he did agree to lend her enough money for the schooling necessary to become a teacher. Stone began teaching at the age of sixteen, earning a dollar a week.

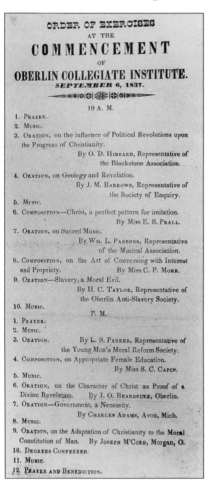

Stone refused to write for her commencement at Oberlin College.

Because her wages were so low, it took her nine years to save enough money for college. The decision of which college to attend was easy because only one accepted women—Oberlin College in Lorain County, Ohio. Oberlin did not deny admission based on race or sex. It was strongly abolitionist and attracted many students from other schools where abolitionism was a forbidden subject.

Stone gave her first public speech at Oberlin. Asked to speak at a celebration of the anniversary of West Indian emancipation, she delivered her speech with confidence and eloquence, thinking nothing of the fact that she was the only female speaker. The next day, however, she was called before the Ladies' Board at the school and reprimanded for her unladylike behavior.

As Stone's graduation approached, several members of her class were elected to speak and write for the commencement ceremony, in accordance with Oberlin tradition. Customarily, the male students were invited to deliver their speeches in person, but the female students were only allowed to write their speeches; faculty members would then read them aloud.

Stone was elected by a large majority to be one of the students to write. But the idea that she was not allowed to present her speech because of her sex outraged her. She prepared a petition to the administration asking that the female students be allowed to speak. Her petition was promptly rejected because the faculty felt it improper for women to participate in public events with men. So Stone decided not to write at all. Several classmates urged her to reconsider, and some of her teachers and even the president of the college spoke to the school administration on her behalf. But the administration refused to bend the rules, and Stone remained steadfast in her position. Thus the commencement ceremony went on without her essay. Several other female students selected to write essays followed Stone's lead and also refused to participate.

Stone made a name for herself before she even finished her education. Noted abolitionist William Lloyd Garrison said of her in a letter to his wife from Oberlin in 1847, the year Stone graduated:

> She is a very superior young woman, and has a soul as free as the air, and is preparing to go forth as a lecturer, particularly in vindication of the rights of women. Her course here has been very firm and independent, and she has caused no small uneasiness to the spirit of sectarianism in the institution.[24]

From Antislavery to Women's Rights

At Oberlin, Stone was exposed to many new ideas and developed her talent for public speaking. Abolitionist in her beliefs since her earliest teaching days, she announced to her family on graduation that she intended to make a career of speaking on behalf of the two causes she cared most about—women's rights and antislavery. In a letter to her mother she wrote:

> There are no trials so great as they suffer who neglect or refuse to do what they believe is their duty. I expect to plead not for the slave only, but for suffering humanity everywhere. Especially do I mean to labor for the elevation of my sex.[25]

Stone was soon employed as a regular lecturer by the Antislavery Society, traveling from city to city speaking on the injustice of slavery. Because abolitionists were often mobbed and sometimes murdered, this required a great deal of courage and dedication. With her clear, powerful, straightforward way of speaking, Stone

A political cartoon showing abolitionists being pummeled with rubbish.

was able to placate many angry crowds. People were amazed that a simple country woman could stand before large, shouting crowds and speak fearlessly with complete conviction.

Nevertheless, no matter where she went, attempts to disrupt her speeches were constant. Sometimes pepper was burned to drive audiences away, or rotten fruit was thrown at her while she spoke. Once, a man in the audience became so agitated that he threw a hymnal at her, hitting her in the head. Another time, someone stuck a hose through a broken pane of glass and sprayed her with water. Stone calmly put on her shawl and continued with her lecture. One time, she arrived at a meetinghouse to find that the crowd consisted mostly of troublemakers. As she began to arrange her antislavery pamphlets on a desk, she was attacked by a storm of spitballs and jeers. She did not react. She simply began her lecture. Before long, the audience was listening to her intently and some people were actually nodding their heads in approval. Many even subscribed to the *Anti-Slavery Standard* afterward and became strong supporters of the cause.

Stone also delivered many speeches on women's rights. The fact that she was a woman who gave public speeches for a living made her words even more convincing. Soon, her reputation spread and people all around the nation were talking about her. Even those who disapproved of a woman speaking in public praised this remarkable speaker. Newspaper articles referred to her as eloquent and gifted. She often tailored her lectures to meet the specific interests of her audience, but no matter what the subject, Stone always employed common sense and sound logic. She began one of her women's rights speeches by saying:

> Perhaps I should say at first here, what to my mind, this Woman's Rights Cause is not. It is not to array the interests of men and women against each other, or create any antagonism between them. It is not to rob man of the rights which are his and give them to woman. . . . We leave our sphere to be made by our capacity.[26]

But soon, Stone got into trouble with the influential Anti-Slavery Society for talking too much about women's rights in her speeches. One night, after she gave a lecture that was supposed to be on abolition but turned into a rally for women's rights, Reverend Samuel May, the general agent of the Anti-Slavery Society, gently told her that her lecture was inappropriate for an antislavery meeting. Stone thought about it and decided that May was absolutely right—she could no longer serve both causes equally. She responded, "Well, Mr. May, I was a woman before I was an abolitionist. I must speak for the women. I will not lecture any more for the Anti-Slavery Society, but will work wholly for women's rights."[27] Thus began Stone's career as a women's rights supporter. She was one of the first women ever to make women's rights her main lecture topic.

Reverend Samuel May, general agent of the Anti-Slavery Society, hired Stone to give speeches about abolition of slavery.

The Woman's Rights Convention and Henry Blackwell

In 1850, Stone helped organize the first national Women's Rights Convention, held in Worcester, Massachusetts. The press made fun of the event, calling it a "motley gathering of fanatical mongrels, of old

Women march to protest "Taxation Without Representation."

grannies, male and female, of fugitive slaves and fugitive lunatics."[28] But for Stone, the convention was inspiring. It was her first encounter with a large number of women who shared her passion for equality and freedom, including many women with whom she would work closely in her future career as a suffragist.

Through this growing circle of like-minded individuals, Stone established many lasting relationships. In 1851 she met Susan B. Anthony when both were in Seneca Falls, New York, to attend a meeting of a group trying to found a coeducational college. The college never came into existence, but Stone and Anthony's meeting developed into a deep friendship. Anthony was already close to Elizabeth Cady Stanton, one of the original women's rights pioneers, but Anthony felt that Stanton's husband and children took too much of her time away from the cause. Anthony was thus especially fond of the independent Stone. Both shared the opinion that marriage was much too compromising for a woman and each had vowed, separately, never to marry and become the property of a man.

But Stone had not counted on meeting Henry Blackwell. Handsome, witty, cultured, and a successful businessman, he was popular with many young women. Like Stone, he had a strong liberal nature and a deep sense of fairness. Blackwell was accustomed to the company of independent, intelligent women. His mother and five sisters were an extraordinary group who had started a school for girls in order to support themselves after Blackwell's father died. One sister, Elizabeth, became one of the first women to meet the qualifications to become a physician in the United States—a remarkable accomplishment at a time when only one school in the entire country agreed to admit her.

Stone had met Henry Blackwell briefly in Cincinnati during one of her lecture tours. Three years later, the two met again at the Worcester convention. This time, Henry firmly resolved that one day they would be married. He and Stone began corresponding regularly, sharing with each other their passion for reform and their ideas about the future.

Stone began staying with Henry's family whenever she was in Cincinnati. She grew fond of the Blackwells and looked forward to her visits with them. They were an intellectual and cultured group, always engaging in lively, stimulating conversation. And although she had made it very clear to Henry that she did not intend to marry, ever, she eagerly anticipated his letters and their occasional meetings. Henry refused to give up, describing a life for them that Stone found hard to resist. After two years, she finally relented and agreed to marry Henry. She was determined, however, not to let her marriage and her new life draw her away from the work that she loved.

Their wedding, on May 1, 1855, attracted a great deal of attention. Instead of becoming Mrs. Henry Blackwell, Stone went against custom and remained Lucy Stone—a shocking breach of convention in those days. In addition, the couple prepared a statement of protest against six specific laws of marriage, which they read and signed at their wedding ceremony. Most local newspapers ridiculed the protest and the marriage.

Although the criticism stung, Stone always maintained that women should be careful not to lose themselves in their husband's identities. To a newspaper reporter, a few months after their marriage, Stone said, "It is an insult to *every man's mother* when *any* woman is written as the relict of any man."[29] In spite of the criticism over their unusual marriage contract, Blackwell and Stone remained happily married until Stone's death thirty-six years later.

A Protest: Taxation Without Representation

For nearly ten years women's rights supporters had argued against "taxation without representation," an idea rooted in the nation's struggle to be free from British rule. Women argued that they should not be expected to pay taxes when they were not considered full citizens under the Constitution. By 1857 this idea was especially important to Stone, who owned the house that she and Henry shared and was required to pay taxes on the property.

In December 1857, while her husband was away on business and she was home in New Jersey with their two-month-old daughter, Alice, Stone wrote a letter to the tax collector:

> Enclosed I return my tax bill, without paying it. My reason for doing so is, that women suffer taxation, and yet have no representation, which is not only unjust to one-half of the adult population, but is contrary to our theory of government. For years some women have been paying their taxes under protest, but still taxes are imposed and representation is not granted.[30]

As a result, the tax collector put up many of Stone's household goods for sale in order to pay the tax debt. Stone told the law officer who performed the sale that he would have to come back and do the same thing every year until the laws for women changed, because she would never voluntarily pay taxes for the support of a government in which she had no voice.

Leader of the AWSA

With the onset of the Civil War, Stone felt an even greater responsibility to lecture, both for women's rights and against slavery. Although she did do some lecturing for abolition, and continued to support both the abolition and women's rights causes, the women's cause soon became overshadowed by the struggle to end the war.

Stone, a pacifist by nature, found the enormous bloodshed of the war foreign and disgusting. It only strengthened her belief in the unfairness of the law toward women. She pointed out to friends and listeners that the government could take any mother's son away to be shot, "and afterwards put its bloody hand in her pocket to help pay the bills."[31] In a letter to her husband, Stone wrote: "I wish this infernal war were over. But the nation does not deserve peace, until it respects human rights."[32]

Nonetheless, Stone did what she could to assist the war effort. She made bandages, as so many women did, and she helped Elizabeth Cady Stanton and Susan B. Anthony organize the National Women's Loyal League to educate women on the political issues surrounding the war and to circulate petitions asking Congress to abolish slavery.

When the war ended in 1865, the Fourteenth Amendment became a major focus for woman suffrage supporters and antislavery supporters alike. The Fourteenth Amendment was designed to give citizenship to all, regardless of race. However, the amendment also introduced the word "male" into the U.S. Constitution for the first time, intentionally excluding women as citizens. It also failed to give black men voting rights.

The exclusion of women from the Fourteenth Amendment convinced Anthony and Stanton that the time had come to work solely for woman suffrage. Stone and some other women's rights supporters disagreed. They felt that they should be loyal to their original mission to achieve suffrage for all citizens, women and black men alike, and merge their efforts with those of the abolitionists to strengthen both causes.

When it became apparent that it was impossible for the two groups of suffragists to work together, they went forward as two separate organizations. One group followed Anthony and Stanton, and the other turned to Stone for leadership. Anthony and Stanton's

Stone asked Mary A. Livermore to serve as editor for her newspaper called the Woman's Journal.

organization became the National Woman Suffrage Association (NWSA) and Stone's became the American Woman Suffrage Association (AWSA). For many years, both organizations worked separately to achieve suffrage for women. Their tactics were different, but their ultimate goal was the same.

The *Woman's Journal*

In 1869, Stone, Blackwell, and their daughter, Alice, moved to Boston. This was an important move for Stone's career as a suffrage leader because the city was home not only to the most influential thinkers and reformers of the time, but also to the New England Woman Suffrage Association, the most active suffrage organization in the country. In Boston, the family was surrounded by like-minded people who were sympathetic to and supportive of the cause.

Stone was also able to realize her long-held dream of starting a publication for women. She was enthusiastic about working for the cause through the paper instead of lecturing, because her travels made it difficult to have a decent family life. She asked Mary A. Livermore, who published her own suffrage and temperance paper, to move to Boston, merge her *Agitator* with the new *Woman's Journal*, and serve as editor. Livermore agreed, and on January 8, 1870, the *Woman's Journal* began publication.

Its masthead read: "A weekly newspaper, published every Saturday in Boston and Chicago, devoted to the interests of woman, to her educational, industrial, legal and political equality, and especially to her right of suffrage."[33]

The eight-page paper featured political articles, news of special concern to women, reports of suffrage activities, poems, stories, book reviews, and tips on cleaning, decorating, and social etiquette. The *Woman's Journal* also sent correspondents to England, Europe, and the Hawaiian Islands to report on women's issues in other parts of the world.

In 1872, Livermore resigned as editor. The majority of the work fell to Stone and Blackwell, who were already extremely busy organizing local women's groups, literary societies, and suffrage rallies, and tending to their daughter. Stone often compared the paper to a big baby that never grew up and always had to be fed. Nonetheless, the paper continued publication and every year attracted a greater following. Eventually, many of the journal articles were reprinted and distributed as pamphlets and booklets to support the cause.

The *Woman's Journal* was published for more than forty-seven years, longer than any other suffrage paper and most other reform papers. In 1917, many years after Stone's death, Carrie Chapman Catt, herself a leader for woman suffrage, paid tribute to the *Woman's Journal*:

> There can be no overestimating the value to the suffrage cause of the *Woman's Journal* in its long and vivid career. It has gone before and it has followed after; it has pointed the way and closed the gaps; it has been history-maker and history-recorder for the suffrage cause. The suffrage success of to-day is not conceivable without the *Woman's Journal's* part in it.[34]

Last Days

Throughout Stone's life, she did an enormous amount of work for women's suffrage, even beyond lecturing and working on the *Woman's Journal*. She led hundreds of organizations, petition drives, arrangements for legislative hearings, conventions, and meetings; met with the press; ran campaigns; wrote and printed tracts; and organized and ran dozens of fund-raising events.

By 1888, when she was seventy years old, Stone's health was declining. Two weeks after what would be Henry's and her final

Alice Stone Blackwell, Lucy's daughter, became editor-in-chief of the Woman's Journal *after her mother's death.*

wedding anniversary in May 1893, Stone and Alice left to speak in front of Congress for woman suffrage. When the congressional sessions were over, Stone made other public appearances to speak for suffrage. But later that summer, in August, when Henry went to Chicago for the annual woman suffrage programs, Stone was too ill to go. In fact, she had stomach cancer and her health would steadily worsen. But she continued to write for the *Woman's Journal* from her sickbed. She also wrote dozens of letters of support and encouragement to other suffrage leaders.

During Stone's last few weeks, the grieving Henry and Alice did nothing but stay near her to offer what comfort they could. Stone died quietly on October 18, at age seventy-five. The *Woman's Journal* of October 21 contained a short tribute to her written by Henry entitled "She Leads Us Still." It also contained a long article by Alice, entitled "A Beautiful Death," in which she wrote:

> On the last afternoon . . . she looked at me and seemed to want to say something. I put my ear to her lips. She said distinctly, "Make the world better." They were almost the last articulate words she uttered. Whether they were a simple exhortation, or part of a sentence the rest of which was inaudible, there was no means of knowing.[35]

After Stone's death, her husband and daughter continued her legacy, working as diligently for women's rights as they had when she was alive. Henry, who survived his wife by sixteen years, served as the editor of the *Woman's Journal* until his death at the age of eighty-four. Alice succeeded Henry as editor in chief of the paper. Alice died in 1950 at the age of ninety-two. She was the only one of the three who lived to witness women receive suffrage.

CHAPTER 5

Anna Howard Shaw (1847–1919): A Woman Pioneer

Anna Howard Shaw was born in Newcastle-on-Tyne, England, in 1847, into a family burdened by great economic hardship. In 1852, when Anna was five years old, her father decided to move his family to America, where he believed they would find prosperity. The Shaw family first settled in New Bedford, Massachusetts, but resided there only for a short time before they moved to Lawrence, Massachusetts, where they lived for the next seven years. There, the Shaw family became involved in the growing abolitionist movement and also associated with several of the many reformers who congregated in the town.

Even at an early age, Anna participated in her family's activities within the abolitionist community. She attended meetings with her parents when she was allowed, and listened intently to their fireside conversations about current issues. One day Anna went into the cellar of her family's home. When she heard a rustling in the coal bin, she investigated and discovered a black woman hiding there. Anna immediately raced up the stairs in excitement to tell her mother what she had seen. Her

Anna Howard Shaw was a minister and physician, as well as a suffragist.

mother, however, silenced Anna at once and sent her directly to bed, fearing that the young girl might not be able to keep the secret. Not until later did Anna learn that her parents had been helping blacks escape slavery by hiding them in the cellar on their way to freedom. This discovery cemented Anna's growing sympathies for the anti-slavery cause.

In 1859, Anna's father decided to move the family once again, this time to the woods of Michigan. Rural life proved to be rough and at times dangerous for a family used to living among the comforts and securities of the city. The Shaws had to contend with potentially dangerous wild animals, as well as the local Indians, both of which caused many a fearful moment. Eventually, however, the Shaw home became known throughout the region as a place where friends and strangers alike could gather for intelligent conversations and exposure to learning. People came from all around to hear Anna's father read aloud from his books.

In this unusual atmosphere of intellectualism and rugged wilderness life, Anna blossomed into an intelligent and sensitive young woman. The influences of her family's alliance with abolitionism and the vast amount of reading she did as a young girl gave her strong opinions about human rights. Anna did not keep her opinions to herself. She frequently preached and lectured to her family or anyone else who would listen.

The Education of a Woman Minister

When Shaw was fifteen years old, she was offered a job teaching the children of her growing wilderness community. The local school was four miles away so Shaw boarded with each student's family in turn. During her first year, she had fourteen students of various ages. There were so few books at the school that the students sometimes had to use church hymnals for their reading lessons.

Shaw was invited to teach for a second year. By this time, the Civil War had begun and her family faced hard times. Her father and brothers, even the youngest, went off to fight in the war, making Shaw the principal supporter of her family for several years. This time instead of boarding with her students, Shaw walked the four miles each way to school and back every day. She and her mother worked themselves ragged; indeed, they worked so hard they fell ill from fatigue. But even though she had little encouragement during those hard years, Shaw was determined that one day she would go to college, and she planned her life according to that dream.

The end of the Civil War brought freedom to Shaw. Finally, she no longer had to put all of her earnings toward maintaining the homestead. With her father and brothers back home, she started to save for her education. Recognizing that it was going to take a very long time to earn enough money for college by teaching, she moved in with her older sister Mary, who lived in Big Rapids, where she planned to earn money by sewing. But after working as a seamstress for only a month, Shaw attended a church service that changed her life. Reverend Marianna Thompson, a female Universalist minister, delivered the sermon. Shaw was so moved by Thompson's words that she herself felt a call to the ministry. After the services, Shaw approached the minister and sought her advice. In her memoirs, *The Story of a Pioneer*, Shaw quotes Thompson's counsel: "My child, give up your foolish idea of learning a trade, and go to school. You can't do anything until you have an education. Get it, and get it now."[36]

Shaw took the advice. She promptly gave up sewing and enrolled in the nearest high school, where she took college preparatory classes. It was during high school that Shaw gave her first sermon. Her participation in school debates, recitations of vast amounts of poetry, and performances in dramatic events attracted the interest of the head elder of her school district. Anxious to be the first elder to have a woman ordained as a Methodist minister, he asked Shaw to preach for him at a local church. Although she had no preaching experience and was only seventeen years old, she agreed.

Soon after, a notice appeared in the local paper reporting the event. When her family learned of it, they were shocked and saddened. Women simply did not pursue the ministry in those days. They offered to pay Shaw's way through college if she gave up the idea. But as much as she wanted to go to college, she knew that she could not turn her back on her calling. She refused their offer.

Shaw continued to preach and study, struggling, as always, to save money for college. Because it was extremely difficult to put any money aside on her small preaching salary, it took her many years to earn the necessary sum. But finally, in 1873, at the age of twenty-five, Shaw entered Albion College in Michigan. Shaw excelled in almost every subject and quickly became involved in one of the college literary groups. She continued to preach, and also gave lectures on temperance to support herself through college.

A Woman Preacher and Doctor

Shaw left Albion after three years to attend the theological school at the University of Boston, where she was the only woman in a class of forty-three. She graduated in 1878, having served almost the whole time as the interim preacher for a Methodist church. Soon after graduation, Shaw's real ministerial career began. She was offered a position as pastor of a church at East Dennis, Cape Cod.

Shaw's duties as pastor began in 1878 and continued for the next seven years. She faced many challenges at East Dennis, beginning upon her arrival, when she found the church members divided into two factions for reasons she never learned. Because Shaw announced to the congregation that she did not want to hear them criticize one another unless it was in writing, the church members began to complain about each other during their public prayers. When Shaw tried to put an end to this practice, one man became so angry over the fact that a mere woman was trying to tell him how to pray that he resigned from the church rather than obey her. Another time, a man explained to Shaw that he didn't attend her church because "There ain't no gal that can teach me nothing."[37] But Shaw convinced him to attend anyway, and he eventually became one of her most loyal supporters.

Ironically, after Shaw left East Dennis years later, some of the men confessed that they rarely attended church after she left. One summed up his feelings by saying:

> When you fust come to us . . . you had a lot of crooked places, an' we had a lot of crooked places; and we kind of run into each other, all of us. But before you left, Sister

East Dennis, Cape Cod, where Shaw had a ministry, probably looked much like this town.

Shaw, why all the crooked places was wore off and everything was as smooth as silk.[38]

Time and again Shaw proved her mettle by standing up for
what she believed. A group of local residents delighted in dancing at her church's annual fair, knowing that dancing was strictly
prohibited by the church's rules. When Shaw learned this group
was again planning to dance, this time at the church's Christmas
fair, she was determined to prevent it. After securing the support
of church officials, Shaw threatened to have anyone who danced
arrested. The would-be dancers were not too worried, intending
to proceed with their plan as soon as Shaw left for the evening.
But Shaw made sure she was the last person to leave, and that
night at least, there was no dancing at the church fair.

Over time, despite such strictness, Shaw became a beloved and
cherished member not only of the church but also the local community. Ultimately, however, she became discontented. She felt she
had done all she could in her role as pastor and that perhaps she
should move on to another calling. In 1882, while still preaching
at East Dennis, Shaw entered the Boston Medical School, where
she received a diploma as a physician in 1885. During her time in
Boston, she met Lucy Stone and her husband, Henry Blackwell,
who together sparked her interest in woman suffrage.

While working toward her degree in medicine, Shaw spent three
nights each week providing health care for the poor. She usually received no money for her services, as her patients were typically too im-
poverished to pay her. Because her most desperate patients were often
women and children, she became acutely aware of the helpless state to
which women were often reduced due to their lack of legal rights.

Her work with the poor, coupled with exposure to woman suffrage leaders like Stone and Blackwell, convinced Shaw that
women needed the vote to use as a tool to improve their status.
Suffrage was soon one of Shaw's dominating interests. Any time
she preached, she mentioned it in her sermon. She addressed it in
her speeches. When she helped patients in the Boston slums, it was
in her bedside conversation. Before long, Shaw's career took a
turn away from the church and toward the suffrage cause. In
1885, Shaw decided to resign her ministry.

The Great Cause

In her ministerial work, Shaw had confronted prejudice against her
based on her sex. She had also experienced the difficulties of a
woman in pursuit of higher education. As a doctor, Shaw had seen
women and children sick, starving, and living in slums because they

Besides lecturing for woman suffrage, Shaw gave speeches for the Woman's Christian Temperance Union.

had been cast off by uncaring husbands. She was ready to do something to improve things for women, and she knew that the changing social climate was making it more important than ever for women to stand up for their rights. She describes this time in her memoirs:

> We were entering upon a deeply significant period. For the first time women were going into industrial competition with men, and already men were intensely resenting their presence. . . . I studied the obtrusive problems of the poor and of the women of the streets; and, looking at the whole social situation from every angle, I could find but one solution for women—the removal of the stigma of disfranchisement. As man's equal before the law, woman could demand her rights, asking favors from no one. With all my heart I joined in the crusade of the men and women who were fighting for her. My real work had begun.[39]

Shaw had begun her career as a women's rights lecturer while still in medical school by speaking occasionally for the Massachusetts Woman Suffrage Association at the invitation of Lucy Stone. Upon leaving the ministry, Shaw lectured full time for the association for two years, and then began to work independently, speaking for both the woman suffrage and temperance causes.

On her lecture tours, Shaw underwent many dramatic experiences. Like so many women's rights supporters who toured and lectured, she was constantly forced to travel all night without rest, to stay in broken-down taverns, and to go without meals. Shaw had life-threatening encounters as well. Once, a group of men who opposed her views on liquor set fire to the building in which she was speaking. Even though everyone made it out safely, Shaw was outraged. But she refused to be defeated, marching her audience to a nearby church where she continued her lecture without incident.

Besides lecturing for woman suffrage, Shaw also spoke for the Woman's Christian Temperance Union. But in 1888, Susan B. Anthony convinced Shaw that she was working too slowly by lecturing for both causes. Anthony told her, "You can't win two causes at once. You're merely scattering your energies. Begin at the beginning. Win suffrage for women, and the rest will follow."[40]

To further persuade Shaw to dedicate herself solely to woman suffrage, Anthony took Shaw on a campaign tour to Kansas. After listening to the strongly persuasive arguments Anthony made night after night at their meetings, Shaw was completely won over. From that point, until Anthony's death eighteen years later, Shaw and Anthony worked side by side for suffrage.

Anthony and Shaw

Shaw and Anthony lectured together, wrote together, and stayed up nights talking together. They spent so much time in each

In an effort to achieve woman suffrage in individual states, Shaw lectured in Kansas, where women often set up suffragist encampments.

other's company that they each developed a unique familiarity with the other's speeches and thoughts. On several occasions, while lecturing, Anthony suffered an attack of throat constriction that forced her to leave the podium in the middle of the lecture. Thanks to the two women's closeness, Shaw was able to resume the speech exactly where Anthony had left off.

From Anthony, Shaw learned to stay calm despite the interruptions, annoyances, and outright disasters that frequently occurred during their speaking tours. Anthony was the master of maintaining professionalism and dignity throughout any situation. The two women traveled throughout the states campaigning in all kinds of weather and conditions. Often they had to sleep on the dirt floors of local farmers. Sometimes they barely had enough water to drink, much less bathe in. And more often than not, they faced angry, insulting crowds. Nonetheless, every night Anthony would remind Shaw of their great mission. No matter how bleak their situation, Anthony could always inspire Shaw with her strong fighting spirit.

Shaw Heads NAWSA

In 1892, Shaw was elected vice president of NAWSA. Although she served in that office for over twelve years, her most significant work for the organization came after 1904, when she was elected president after Carrie Chapman Catt's resignation. Shaw did not want the presidency at first, but she could not refuse Anthony's entreaties for her to take the position.

Soon after Shaw assumed the NAWSA presidency, Anthony became ill. She would not recover. In her final days, Anthony wanted Shaw with her constantly. Day and night, Shaw stayed by Anthony's bed, holding her hand and watching her grow weaker by the hour. According to Shaw, in her last moments Anthony said:

> I do not know anything about what comes to us after this life ends. But if there is a continuance of life beyond it, and if I have any conscious knowledge of this world and of what you are doing, I shall not be far away from you: and in times of need I will help you all I can. Who knows? Perhaps I may be able to do more for the Cause after I am gone than while I am here.[41]

NAWSA was now entirely in the hands of Shaw and her administration.

Early in her presidency, Shaw focused her efforts on achieving woman suffrage in individual states. She began by working in Oregon,

Washington, and then California. In 1912, Shaw launched the largest campaign that NAWSA had ever undertaken, working in six states in which state constitutional amendments were expected to pass: Ohio, Michigan, Wisconsin, Oregon, Arizona, and Kansas.

During this vigorous campaign, Shaw gave four and five speeches a day, sometimes to rather rowdy audiences. But her gift for speaking and talent for winning over the toughest crowds nearly always tamed her listeners. Once, she held a meeting in the street during a "roundup" festival in Oregon in which thousands of Indians, cowboys, and ranchers were riding around blowing horns, shouting, and singing. Somehow, Shaw managed to get their attention and soon, a crowd gathered trying to hear her speech. In her memoirs, Shaw writes: "Never have we had more courteous or enthusiastic listeners than those wild and happy horsemen. Best of all, they not only cheered our sentiments, but they followed up their cheers with their votes."[42]

Shaw campaigned vigorously with the help of supporters like those seen here, mounting a poster for woman suffrage.

Shaw's Final Work for Women

In Shaw's years as NAWSA president, its membership grew from seventeen thousand to more than two hundred thousand. Under her leadership, the association waged five to ten campaigns each year, as opposed to the one campaign in ten years that the association had previously undertaken. The campaign strategy during her presidency consisted primarily of making speeches throughout the states that were on the verge of granting woman suffrage. As part of each campaign, Shaw herself made speeches in the major cities of almost every state the organization targeted.

Shaw felt it was especially valuable to speak to audiences of men whenever possible. She delivered one memorable speech to

Shaw speaks to a group outside her home in Sea Cliff, Long Island, N.Y.

the retired soldiers living in the Soldier's Home at Leavenworth in Kansas. She entertained the men with stories of how she and her mother and sisters had been left in a rugged cabin in the wilderness until her father and older brothers could join them, when her family first moved to Michigan. She related how, as pioneer children, she and her younger brother plowed the fields, hauled water from a far-off creek, and tapped trees for sap.

These stories of her family's struggle to set up a homestead in the Michigan wilderness struck a chord with male and female audiences alike. After warming her listeners up with these colorful anecdotes, Shaw usually found her ideas on woman suffrage greeted with approval and applause.

But in spite of her ability to win over her listeners with charming stories and powerful ideas, she still faced a constant barrage of opposition. During a convention in Atlanta, a prominent local minister preached a sermon warning members of his church to keep away from the suffrage meetings. Playing on the prejudices held by some members of his congregation, he claimed that the suffragists did not care about woman suffrage as much as they did about interracial marriage. He also berated the suffragists for trying to break up homes and demoralize women.

Though damaging to the cause, these criticisms were not new. Although the suffrage cause was becoming better understood with time, Shaw and the other suffragists were constantly confronted with these and other arguments that suffragists before them had also faced. To one common argument Shaw responded:

> You men say that we will neglect our families if we vote. You state that we will grow coarse and not be attractive to you; you say that we will always cast our ballot wrongly. Very well! Does the government demand of a man, when he starts to vote, that he shall promise not to neglect his family, that he will stay attractive to the other sex and always cast his vote right?[43]

Despite the opposition, the suffragists continued to make progress. Ten states gave women the right to vote during Shaw's NAWSA presidency.

Shaw resigned as NAWSA president in 1915, but her suffrage work did not end. In 1917 she accepted the position of chairman of the Women's Committee for the Council of National Defense, in which she worked to coordinate women's activities during World War I. She also continued to speak on behalf of woman suffrage at every opportunity, in addition to preaching whenever invited.

Shaw (center) campaigned tirelessly as president of the National American Woman Suffrage Association.

Shaw worked tirelessly for women's rights until her dying day, just as Susan B. Anthony and Elizabeth Cady Stanton had before her. She died on July 2, 1919, just as she was making plans to set out on a speaking tour in support of President Woodrow Wilson's peace treaty, less than a year before women finally gained the right to vote. At Shaw's memorial service, Carrie Chapman Catt, who both preceded and succeeded Shaw as NAWSA president, said of her: "Likewise the fire of inspiration, kindled in the great soul of Anna Howard Shaw, touched into flame the zeal and courage of her messengers who in turn reached the homes of all races, all faiths with her fervor and power."[44]

CHAPTER 6

Alice Paul (1885–1977): A Militant Leader

Like Susan B. Anthony, Alice Paul, born in Moorestown, New Jersey, on January 11, 1885, was raised a Quaker. Once asked what converted her to the woman suffrage cause, Paul responded that she could not remember when she did not believe in it. "You know," she said, "the Quakers have always believed in woman suffrage."[45] The Quakers believed that not only were women equal to men before God, they were obligated to become involved in social reform.

Alice's childhood was uncommonly serious—no music or dance was allowed in the Paul household. Instead she was encouraged to read, study, and become educated on current social issues. Later in her life, when questioned about her childhood, Paul claimed to have forgotten most of it. Many of her closest friends and colleagues say that she worked too hard to stop and recall her past.

Alice Paul was a passionate leader for woman suffrage.

One thing that is known about Paul's family is that they believed strongly in education, and encouraged Paul in her many academic pursuits. Paul steadily acquired formal degrees—a B.A. from Swarthmore in 1905, an M.A. from the University of Pennsylvania in 1907, and a Ph.D. from the same university in 1912. Her studies focused on social work and the law, fueling a passionate interest in human rights.

During her time as a student, Paul was involved in numerous charity and educational outreach organizations through which she worked primarily with the poor in immigrant neighborhoods. Paul said later that the plight of the desperate people with whom she came in contact filled her with a deep sense of sadness and hopelessness. Although she wanted to pursue whatever means she could to help the poor, she realized early on that she could not find real satisfaction in doing so through social work. Because most of the poor people she encountered were women, Paul eventually took up the work of advocating women's rights. Her background in social work, along with her legal studies, gave her the knowledge and experience to become one of the suffrage movement's most passionate leaders.

Suffragists in England

In 1912, Paul traveled to England to continue her studies. There, she was invited to join the Pankhurst forces, a group of suffragists

Emmeline Pankhurst (right) and her daughter formed the Pankhurst forces in England, inspiring Paul to take more decisive action in the woman suffrage movement in the United States.

lead by Emmiline Pankhurst. The Pankhurst forces employed militant tactics—such as picketing, hunger striking, and parading—to promote their message, and were frequently arrested and jailed for their actions. Initially, Paul was only a passive supporter of the suffrage cause in England, but once she joined the Pankhurst forces, she became convinced that suffrage could be won only by taking decisive action, including civil disobedience. Eventually, Paul herself was arrested and jailed many times for her participation in suffrage campaigns. Her first ar-

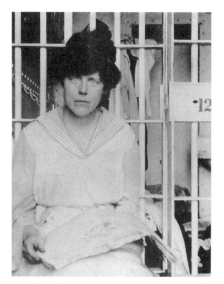

Paul's friend Lucy Burns, with whom she was jailed in England on several occasions.

rest, shortly before she was scheduled to return to the United States, was for demonstrating for suffrage in front of Parliament. She was quickly released but soon arrested again after trying to speak for woman suffrage at a protest meeting. This time, she was sentenced to two weeks in jail, where she went on a hunger strike that lasted over five days until at last the authorities gave up and released her.

In England, Paul befriended another American suffragist, Lucy Burns. The two worked in the Pankhurst forces together and were jailed together on a number of occasions. In the summer of 1912, Burns returned to America and Paul visited her on Long Island. For some time, Paul had been pondering the suffrage situation in the United States. She felt American suffragists should forget about working for amendments to each of the state constitutions and instead focus on amending the federal Constitution to give women nationwide the right to vote.

Paul and Burns devised a plan to work for a constitutional amendment in Washington. They took their proposal to Anna Howard Shaw, Harriot Stanton Blatch, and Mary Ware Dennett, the leaders of the National American Woman Suffrage Association (NAWSA). The NAWSA leaders agreed to implement Burns and Paul's plan by sponsoring the Congressional Committee. Headed by Paul, the committee was to be dedicated to raising funds to campaign for a federal amendment. The establishment of the Congressional Committee marked the beginning of Paul's suffrage work in America.

A Dramatic Suffrage Parade

On March 3, 1913, the eve of President Woodrow Wilson's first inauguration, Paul, now as head of the Congressional Committee, led a group of suffragists in a demonstration that attracted a great deal of attention to the American suffrage cause. Nearly eight thousand women marched in a parade that began at the Capitol and ended at the Hall of the Daughters of the American Revolution. They carried a banner that read:

WE DEMAND AN AMENDMENT TO THE CONSTITUTION OF
THE UNITED STATES ENFRANCHISING THE WOMEN OF THE
COUNTRY.[46]

Though the demonstrators had obtained a legal permit to march, the police did nothing to protect them against the angry mob of objectors that moved in on them. The police appeared, in fact, to ignore the violence that ensued, resulting in severe injuries to some of the suffragists. Not until the secretary of war called in troops from Fort Meyer was order restored.

Although this incident was frightening for Paul and the other participants, it caused a public stir that nearly overshadowed the inauguration of the president. Recognizing the power of publicity, from this point on Paul and her group made it a policy to keep people "watching the suffragists" by doing whatever it took to get their attention.

The Congressional Committee

Through the Congressional Committee, Paul put her influential personality and organizational skills to work. One of the first things she did was obtain a headquarters from which the committee could operate. It was located on F Street near the fashionable Willard Hotel, where it was highly visible to the public. The headquarters started out as one rented room, but after only one year it grew to ten rooms. Eventually, the headquarters would take up two entire floors.

Volunteers performed nearly all of the work at the committee headquarters. Paul's decisive leadership and convincing manner enabled her to persuade anyone who stopped by to pitch in and work. Those who worked with her said that she was driven by a "fury of speed," that she was a "human dynamo." Some claimed that Paul never sat still long enough take off her hat and coat. Winifred Mallon, a suffragist who worked closely with Paul, said: "I worked with Alice Paul for three months before

Nearly eight thousand women marched in a parade on the eve of President Woodrow Wilson's inauguration to attract attention to woman suffrage in the United States.

I saw her with her hat off. I was perfectly astonished, I remember, at the mass of hair. I had never suspected its existence."[47]

In addition to her energy and dedication, Paul's colleagues praised her knowledge of politics and her ability to negotiate with politicians and other influential individuals.

Besides fund-raising to support the suffrage effort, the Congressional Committee organized a series of classes to educate women about suffrage. The classes were held indoors and outdoors, sometimes numbering as many as ten a day. Often, information was presented in the form of skits or dramatic performances to attract women otherwise disinterested in politics. In November 1913, the committee also began publication of the *Suffragist*, which reported on the group's activities. The publication also included editorials, essays, and cartoons, all dedicated to the issue of woman suffrage.

Paul Influences President Wilson

In response to the notorious suffrage parade that preceded his inauguration, President Wilson often tried to show public support for woman suffrage, but in reality he did nothing substantial to further the cause. Paul once described an interaction she had with Wilson by saying that he "was as he always was . . . he gave the impression of being very scholarly, very tolerant and respectful and completely in accord with the idea that women could vote."[48] But in truth, President Wilson knew very little about woman suffrage until Paul and her committee made it a priority to educate him.

Seven days after his inauguration, Wilson announced that a special session of Congress would be held on April 7. The Congressional Committee promptly asked the president to recommend the Suffrage Amendment during the session. In an effort to win him over, the committee arranged a series of meetings with Wilson. At the first, held on March 17, he admitted that he had never been very concerned about suffrage.

The committee sent a delegate to meet with Wilson again on March 28. This time Wilson informed the suffragists that the upcoming special session of Congress would be too occupied with other issues to consider woman suffrage. Even after a third meeting on March 31, much to the suffragists' disappointment, Wilson reiterated that Congress would not consider the Suffrage Amendment.

The committee continued to arrange marches to draw media and official attention, including one to take place on the opening day of the special session. Paul and other committee members had also spent weeks before the special session writing to the congressmen, urging them to introduce a Suffrage Amendment.

On the opening day of the special session, suffragists from each of the 435 congressional districts assembled in Washington, each marching behind her state banner. When the marchers arrived at the doors of Congress, they were greeted by many supportive congressmen. Soon after the women had taken their places in the galleries of the Senate and the House, the Suffrage Amendment was introduced. Despite what Wilson had said, their request for consideration had finally been granted. This was the second time the amendment had been introduced to Congress since 1878.

With the Suffrage Amendment once again before Congress, Paul decided to disband the Congressional Committee and reorganize as the Congressional Union (CU), made up of representatives from throughout the country. The CU would be concerned with raising funds to continue the campaigning started by the Congressional Committee. The official policy statement of the CU read:

President Woodrow Wilson gives a speech. He knew little about woman suffrage until Paul made it her priority to educate him.

[Our] policy will be called militant and in a sense it is, being strong, positive and energetic. If it is militant to appeal to women to use their vote to bring suffrage to this country, then it is militant to appeal to men or women to use their vote to any good end.[49]

But the CU was made up primarily of younger women who were relative newcomers to the suffrage movement, and the older women in NAWSA were not always comfortable with the union's aggressive tactics. They especially disagreed with the CU's employment of the British model of campaigning, in which the members opposed the party in office to protest the government's unfairness to women. NAWSA had historically operated as a nonpartisan organization, showing neither support for nor opposition toward any political party. Eventually, tactical differences between Paul and Anna Howard Shaw, the president of NAWSA, led to the CU's separation from its parent group. But Alice Paul remained at its helm.

The National Woman's Party Emerges

In 1916, Paul used the CU to found the National Woman's Party during a meeting held in Chicago. About the party, which attracted strong and motivated women from all backgrounds, Paul wrote:

The Woman's Party had from beginning to end—every kind of woman. . . . Women of every experience and every walk of life you find have this same feeling for building up respect for their own sex, power for their own sex, and lifting it up out of a place where there is contempt for women in general. . . . Some people are just born feminists.[50]

The party kicked off its organization with a series of picketing protests aimed at defeating President Wilson in the fall election. These protests continued throughout the year, but Wilson was reelected nonetheless. When the president addressed Congress that year, members of the Woman's Party slipped into seats in the gallery and, as he began to speak, unveiled a banner advocating suffrage. They also distributed press releases urging the public to stop supporting the president since he didn't support suffrage for women.

Besides actively opposing the president, some members of the Woman's Party provoked arrest as a means of attracting more attention to the suffrage cause. In jail, many of the women went on hunger strikes. The newspapers were filled with stories of the pain they endured while jailers jammed tubes down their throats to try to force them to eat. At one point, Paul herself was even placed in a psychiatric hospital and treated for mental illness because of her unwillingness to cooperate with the authorities. Incidents of this nature generated a great deal of sympathy for the suffrage cause.

However, the militant behavior of the Woman's Party only served to emphasize its differences with NAWSA. NAWSA began to distance itself even more from the Woman's Party, particularly after Paul and her group burned an image of the president in front of the White House—an aggressive action that NAWSA wanted nothing to do with.

For its part, the Woman's Party felt that its bold actions had made a great deal of progress for women's suffrage. They considered the NAWSA leaders old-fashioned and passive. Paul and other Woman's Party workers felt that they deserved credit for reenergizing the suffrage cause. Their group, they argued, was the one that showed enough courage to be arrested and jailed, while the NAWSA women were too timid to be effective.

NWP Watchfires

On Christmas Day 1918, Paul implemented a new action for the Woman's Party—to keep a fire burning on the pavement in front of the White House until Congress passed the Suffrage Amendment. Wood for the bonfire was to be sent in from every state. In addition, whenever the president made a speech in war-torn Europe to plead for democracy, a copy of the speech would be burned in the bonfire. At the same time, a bell above the party headquarters' door would toll.

When the initial fire was lit, a banner displayed next to it read:

PRESIDENT WILSON IS DECEIVING THE WORLD WHEN HE
APPEARS AS THE PROPHET OF DEMOCRACY.
PRESIDENT WILSON HAS OPPOSED THOSE WHO DEMAND
DEMOCRACY FOR THIS COUNTRY.
HE IS RESPONSIBLE FOR THE DISFRANCHISEMENT OF
MILLIONS OF AMERICANS.
WE IN AMERICA KNOW THIS.
THE WORLD WILL FIND HIM OUT.[51]

This fire would be the first of many "Watchfires of Freedom" ignited by the Woman's Party. This first occasion, however, ignited more than wood. The display enraged a group of soldiers and sailors, who tipped over the urn holding the fire and began to stamp out the blazing embers. The instigators of the fire—Paul, Julia Emory, Hazel Hunkins, and Edith Ainge—were all arrested.

While these four suffragists were being taken to jail, others rekindled the fire. Paul, who was detained at the police station only for a short time, returned to the fire and stayed with it through the night. The fire kept burning. On the third day, another group of

National Woman's Party members protest the jailing of women who demanded woman suffrage.

sailors violently attacked the suffragists. They tore the banner, broke the urn, and tore up several other flags that were displayed. But, once the attack was over, the women again rekindled the fire and calmly continued their watch. The suffragists kept the fire going, in spite of its being stamped out and kicked about a number of times. Occasionally, the women keeping watch would be arrested and sometimes jailed. Any time one of them was placed in jail, she immediately began a hunger strike to protest her imprisonment.

These arrests, imprisonment, and rekindled fires continued for many weeks. In the meantime, the Woman's Party, continuing its policy of seeking publicity, sent a group of speakers who had served prison sentences throughout the country on tour. The car in which they traveled was called the Prison Special, and the newspapers nicknamed the women the Prison Specialists. Whenever the women gave speeches, they wore replicas of their prison uniforms.

Protest at the New York Metropolitan Opera House

On February 24, 1919, the president returned from Europe, where he had been meeting with allies about postwar issues. Paul and the rest of the Woman's Party were waiting for him when he arrived in Boston. They waved banners and carried signs that read:

MR. PRESIDENT, HOW LONG MUST WOMEN WAIT FOR LIBERTY?
MR. PRESIDENT, WHAT WILL YOU DO FOR WOMAN SUFFRAGE?[52]

The police asked the women to leave, but they refused. Eventually, they were arrested. However, they had once again attracted publicity for their cause.

When he arrived back in the capital, the president immediately scheduled a meeting to discuss the Suffrage Amendment. Despite Wilson's growing signs of support for the amendment, it did not pass before the next session of Congress adjourned. Shortly after the session was dismissed, President Wilson made plans to travel to Europe again. On the way, he was to make one stop in New York to speak at the Metropolitan Opera House. When Paul found out, she planned a massive demonstration to take place outside the Opera House.

So, on the evening of March 4, 1919, a long line of suffragists marched from the headquarters of the Woman's Party to the Opera House at Fortieth Street and Broadway. On their way, they were blocked by a barricade of more than a hundred police. When

Paul's Woman's Party constantly pressured President Wilson to respond to the demand for woman suffrage.

the suffragists tried to continue on, hundreds of police and military officers rushed upon them, pushing them back and breaking the banners they carried.

Several of the women, including Paul, were arrested but released shortly thereafter. They returned to the Woman's Party headquarters and resumed their march to the Opera House. Once again, the police rushed them and trampled many of the women, who were found bruised and bleeding afterward. About the incident, suffragist Doris Stevens wrote:

> Not a word was spoken by a single officer of the 200 policemen in the attack to indicate the nature of our offense. Clubs were raised and lowered and the women beaten back with such cruelty as none of us had ever witnessed before . . . women were knocked down and trampled under foot, some of them almost unconscious, others bleeding from the hands and face; arms were bruised and twisted; pocket-books were snatched and wrist-watches stolen.[53]

Ultimately, the police succeeded in pushing the women all the way back to party headquarters. Later that night, the headquarters was broken into and vandalized by angry mobs who tore down banners and burned the suffrage flags stored within.

The massive protest received a great deal of attention and the abusive behavior of the police and military officers stirred the public's sympathies for the suffragists. With public opinion turning in their favor, Paul and the other Women's Party leaders knew that the Suffrage Amendment had a very good chance of passage before the next session of Congress adjourned. The constant pressure they had placed on Wilson and his party was working. The president finally got serious about woman suffrage, especially after the Opera House protest generated so much publicity. Wilson began to push the senators who were still ambivalent about woman suffrage to vote for the Suffrage Amendment.

And so it was that finally, after years of pickets and protests, the Suffrage Amendment giving women the right to vote was passed in 1920. In "Revelations of a Woman Lobbyist," Maud Younger, Paul's friend and a member of the Woman's Party, describes the group's reaction to the final passage: "We walked slowly homeward, talking a little, silent a great deal. This was the day toward which women had been struggling for more than half a century! We were in the dawn of woman's political power in America."[54]

Upon passage of the Suffrage Amendment, Paul said:

American women stand with the vote, won at the cost of millions of dollars, of priceless energy, health and even of life, ready at last to take their share in the burdens and the responsibilities of self government. Our victory cannot be a

Alice Paul, seen here at the National Woman's Party Headquarters, receives congratulations on the passage of the Nineteenth Amendment.

signal for rest. It is not only the symbol of the new status which women have earned, but also the tool with which they must end completely all discrimination against them in departments of life outside the political realm.[55]

Paul's work for women's suffrage was finished, but she still felt that she had more work to do for women. She continued to advocate women's rights and eventually went back to school to further her law studies. In 1923, at a convention of the National Woman's Party, she proposed the Equal Rights Amendment (ERA), which said that "no right shall be denied or abridged by either the federal or local government on account of sex." Although Congress passed the ERA in 1972, the amendment failed to win ratification. Paul continued to fight for the ERA until her death on July 9, 1977.

CHAPTER 7

Carrie Chapman Catt (1859–1947): "The Winning Plan"

Carrie Chapman Catt once described her younger self as "an ordinary child in an ordinary family on an ordinary farm."[56] Yet from this modest beginning, she would go on to become the suffrage movement's master planner whose strategies would finally, after decades of work, bring about the passage of the women's suffrage amendment.

Carrie was born on February 9, 1859, in Ripon, Wisconsin. When she was seven, her family moved to the small rural town of Charles City, Iowa. During the presidential election of 1872, her family favored the editor and reformer Horace Greeley, who was running against Ulysses S. Grant. When Carrie's father and the family's hired man prepared to go vote, Carrie asked her mother why she too wasn't dressing to go. Her mother answered that she wasn't going. A surprised Carrie asked, "Then how are you going to vote for Greeley?"[57] and her whole family laughed. To the smart and strong-willed Carrie, however, the fact that women could not vote was no laughing matter.

During her junior year in high school, Carrie approached her father about attending Iowa State Agricultural College once she graduated. She knew that, like most farmers, he did not have a lot of ready cash, so she had already worked out a plan to pay for it. If he would give her $25 a year, she would earn the rest—$125— by teaching during the summer.

When Carrie graduated from college in 1880, she was the only woman among nineteen graduates. Young, energetic, and ambitious, she planned to become a lawyer, a profession that was just opening to women. Carrie began to read law books in the office of a Charles City attorney. But a year later, she received an offer to teach high school in Mason City for $40 a month. She accepted the offer in order to earn money for law school. She was so highly appreciated that when, in her second year of teaching, the combined principal and superintendent of the city schools left midterm, Carrie's students signed a petition requesting that she replace him. So instead of going to law school, she continued to teach and to serve as principal.

Catt Becomes a Suffragist

In March 1883, the same month that Catt was promoted to principal, a man named Leo Chapman purchased the Mason City weekly *Republican* and began to serve as its editor. Chapman was an attractive twenty-six-year-old who did not smoke or drink and who strongly advocated temperance and woman suffrage. It did not take long for Catt and Chapman to meet and become friends. Because they were both very involved in the community, they soon found themselves working together on many town projects.

On February 12, 1885, Catt and Chapman were married at her home in Charles City. At the time, women could teach only if they were unmarried, so Catt left her teaching position to work with her husband as coeditor of the *Republican*. Catt added a section called "Woman's World" to the paper. In this section she listed notable achievements of women, wrote articles on a woman's right to strike for better pay and working conditions, published notes of feminist interest from other publications, and reminded readers of the need to work for woman suffrage.

Catt attended her first woman's conference in October of that same year in Des Moines. There, Catt met many of the most influential women in the nation, including astronomer and professor Maria Mitchell; Clara Colby, editor of the *Woman's Tribune*; and Ellen Foster, one of the first women to be certified to practice law in Iowa. Catt also heard Lucy Stone speak for woman suffrage. Impressed by the intelligence and strong character of these women, Catt referred to them in the report

Carrie Chapman Catt attended her first woman's conference in October of 1885.

she wrote for the *Republican* as "the strongest, best-educated, most earnest, broad-minded and philosophical women in the United States."[58] Later that month, inspired by the conference, Catt gathered a few friends and went house-to-house through Mason City to gather signatures for a petition in support of woman suffrage, to be presented to the state legislature in 1886.

In early 1886, the Chapmans sold the *Republican* and made plans to move to California. In May, Leo went ahead to scout things out, while Catt stayed with her parents in Charles City, planning to join him when he sent for her. Instead, in August, a telegram came from San Francisco saying that Chapman was very ill with typhoid fever. Catt left on the first train but by the time she arrived in California, Chapman had died.

Writing and Lecturing

The year that followed Chapman's death was one of the darkest periods in Catt's life. In addition to grief over her loss, she was faced with enormous financial problems. The sale of the *Republican* had left her with very little funds, and what she did have had gone for her husband's burial expenses. In her desperation to earn some money, she took whatever writing jobs she could find. She wrote ads and freelance articles, and did any kind of reporting work that was offered.

This experience exposed Catt firsthand to the cruelties suffered by women in the working world. She frequently found herself the victim of sexual harassment and discrimination. One evening, a businessman that Catt was interviewing made advances toward her; when she refused him, he rushed at her and grabbed her. She escaped, but her feelings of anger and embarrassment persisted for months afterward.

During her struggle to find work, Carrie ran into George Catt, a classmate from college. Since she had last seen him, he had become a civil engineer for a San Francisco bridge-building firm. George pointed out that public speaking was very popular and might be a good way for her to make money, especially since she had been such a skilled speaker in school. Carrie liked the idea and soon she had written three lectures and hired an agent to schedule appearances for her. She stayed in San Francisco long enough to perfect and deliver her speeches, then she returned to Charles City to begin her new lecturing career.

Back in Charles City, though her lectures were extremely popular and she was quite busy, she still made time to edit the *Floyd*

County Advocate and join the Woman's Christian Temperance Union, the only local organization that supported woman suffrage. Eventually, an Iowa suffrage leader discovered Catt and asked her to be the organizer for woman suffrage in Floyd County. Catt jumped at this opportunity and was soon elected to be the recording secretary at the state convention. She began speaking on woman suffrage much more frequently, and after only one year, she had started over ten new woman suffrage clubs. She was elected the Iowa delegate to the convention of the National American Woman Suffrage Association in Washington, D.C.

After the convention, Carrie headed to the Northwest on a speaking tour. But lecturing was not her only reason for the trip. In Seattle, on June 10, 1890, she married George Catt, who was now in charge of the San Francisco Bridge Company. He was in Seattle to direct the rebuilding of the piers, bridges, and waterfront structures that had been destroyed during a fire that had consumed almost the entire city.

The couple made an unusual and extremely compatible match. They were both extraordinarily talented in their own ways and they each supported the other's goals. About their marriage, Carrie said:

> We made a team to work for the cause. My husband used to say that he was as much a reformer as I, but that he couldn't work at reforming and earn a living at the same time; but what he could do was to earn living enough for two and free me from all economic burden, and thus I could reform for two. That was our bargain and we happily understood each other.[59]

In 1892, George's career took them to the east coast for a project in Boston. They moved in time for Catt to attend the annual NAWSA convention in Washington, D.C. There, Susan B. Anthony—who had been sizing up the talented, hardworking Catt for some time—appointed her to head a new business committee for NAWSA. Catt's responsibilities were to recruit and educate new suffragists. She had to hire speakers, plan trips, make arrangements for the speakers, and raise money.

Catt Is Elected President of NAWSA

As head of the business committee, Catt was quick to implement many of her ideas to increase support. One of her first actions was to call the first ever Mississippi Valley Conference, which was held in Des Moines in September 1892. Catt knew how important it

While serving as president of the National American Woman Suffrage Association, Catt attended this Congressional Convention held in N.Y.

was for women to meet and share ideas, yet very few midwestern women were able to attend the national women's conferences that were held in Washington, D.C.

In 1894, Catt and Anthony headed to the South in response to suffragists there, who had been requesting support from the national organization for some time. While on tour, Catt realized that the NAWSA had some major weaknesses that needed to be corrected if they were going to succeed. Over the years the NAWSA had become disorganized and unfocused—there were lots of meetings and rallies, but very little planning and forecasting. Catt felt that the time had come to reorganize. They needed to come up with new strategies and act immediately to raise some money.

Once the tour of the South was finished, Catt headed a new Organization Committee. Her main objective for the committee was to coordinate the southern and western states and territories so that they would all be working together for a common goal—ultimately, the Sixteenth Amendment—instead of working separately for suffrage in their own states only. She also developed a "Course of Study" to educate suffragists in political science so that they could speak intelligently about political issues.

In 1895, Catt made a trip west. During her visit, Utah became the third state to allow woman suffrage. George Catt reported the Utah success to the NAWSA convention in his wife's absence. Soon, victory came again, this time in Idaho. But after these successes came a long dry spell in which the suffrage movement struggled along lamely. In fact, the efforts over the next fourteen years amounted to little more than a feeble attempt to keep the original ideas of woman suffrage alive.

But Catt did not give up. Instead, she worked even harder, realizing that the suffragists had to keep their spirits up or the whole movement would fail. She traveled from city to city and state to state to revive dying clubs and to reenergize discouraged suffragists. Catt used small victories to inspire suffragists across the nation. In 1899, she suggested that NAWSA publish a Woman's Century Calendar in which every year of the century was marked by an event important to the women's movement.

Catt's work on the Organization Committee made her the most logical candidate to replace Susan B. Anthony as president of NAWSA. When Anthony resigned the presidency in 1900, she nominated Catt for the position, and Catt was elected by a unanimous vote.

Internationalism

Soon after Catt was elected president of NAWSA, she started work to create an international woman suffrage organization. There already existed the International Council of Women (ICW) with over a million members worldwide. The ICW, however, supported many

In 1904, the International Council of Women was held in Berlin. In that same year Catt resigned as president of the National American Woman Suffrage Association in order to focus her attention on international work for women's rights.

issues—peace, education, sanitation—that were not exclusively women's issues. Thus, suffrage did not get the attention Catt thought it needed.

Catt began by planning the first meeting to be held at the annual NAWSA convention in Washington, D.C. She sent out a questionnaire to countries all over the world. She asked about the rights of married and unmarried women, about women's jobs and wages, if women could hold meetings and speak in public, and whether women could vote or hold office. She received responses from thirty-two countries. The answers painted a bleak picture of women's rights throughout the world. As a result of her inquiry, on February 12, 1902, Catt organized the International Woman Suffrage Alliance (IWSA). Seven of the eight countries with woman suffrage societies were represented: Australia, Denmark, Germany, Great Britain, Norway, Sweden, and the United States. Suffragists also attended from Chile, Hungary, Russia, Turkey, and Switzerland.

In 1904, Catt resigned her position as president of NAWSA in order to focus her attention on international work. Then, in 1905, her husband died of complications from gallstones. For several months, Catt was too grief-stricken to work for woman suffrage at all. But eventually, she decided to pick up her work where she

Catt organized the International Woman Suffrage Alliance with Great Britain as a member. British suffragists stand beside a trolley surrounded by signs encouraging women's right to vote.

had left off and began to plan the third IWSA meeting in Copenhagen. That year, in 1906, four more countries joined the IWSA: Canada, Hungary, Italy, and Russia.

In 1907, Catt experienced another personal loss when her brother Will died. His death was so devastating to Catt's mother, Maria, that her own health failed and she, too, died. This double tragedy took a heavy toll on Catt. She stayed in Iowa with her older brother and his wife until mid-January 1908 to recover. But soon, she was once again making arrangements for the upcoming IWSA meeting in Amsterdam.

Catt delivered the opening statements at the hearing in Amsterdam. In her speech she made the point that the women's movement could not be considered a success until women's history became a part of the world's history. She emphasized the challenges that modern economics were bringing to the women's rights struggle. In her address she said:

> Modern conditions are pushing hundreds of thousands of women out of their homes into the labor market. Everywhere paid less than men for equal work, everywhere discriminated against, they are utterly at the mercy of forces over which they have no control.[60]

By 1908, four more countries had joined the IWSA alliance: Bulgaria, Finland, South Africa, and Switzerland. Many of the countries were reporting progress. Twenty-two national parliaments and twenty-nine state legislatures had been petitioned for woman suffrage.

Catt's Winning Plan

Until 1913, Catt had been mostly concerned with her international work. She traveled abroad whenever she could and attended every IWSA convention. But in 1913, she began to spend more time in the United States, working especially to gain support for suffrage in the state of New York. With the largest population in the nation, the state had the greatest number of representatives, making it very important to the suffrage cause.

Then in 1915, Anna Howard Shaw announced her resignation as president of NAWSA. Catt was the logical replacement, and though she did not want the job because she was afraid it would interfere with her IWSA work, she agreed to be reelected. Her first step as president was to reacquaint herself with as many suffragists as she could, feeling that she had grown out of touch with them in the twelve years since her previous presidency. She went to state conventions, conferences, and meetings and even visited individual suffragists at their homes.

Next, Catt called a meeting with the presidents of the state suffrage associations, where she laid out the organization's new strategy. The main objective was to achieve passage of the federal suffrage amendment by pursuing four main goals: one, get resolutions from each state legislature to Congress; two, push for a referendum or a popular vote in states where there was a chance of getting a constitutional amendment; three, ask each state to give women whatever suffrage they could, preferably rights to vote in

As depicted in this political cartoon, public opinion during WWI embraced woman suffrage.

presidential elections; and four, in the South, push for rights to vote in the primary elections. These goals became known as Catt's "Winning Plan." Catt herself called it a "new deal."

In 1917, the United States finally entered World War I, and the war dominated American politics for most of the next two years. Catt personally opposed war for any reason. But as American involvement grew near, Catt urged suffragists to support the government in whatever way they could:

I am myself a pacifist, now and forever. War is to my mind a barbarism, a relic of the stone age, but I hold that that belief has nothing to do with the present sit-

Catt marches in a New York parade urging support for woman suffrage.

uation. Whether we approve or disapprove, war is here. It is not the appeal of war but the call of civilization which is summoning women to new duties and responsibilities.[61]

Meanwhile, Catt continued to put her Winning Plan in motion. It started to reap results in January 1917, when North Dakota awarded women the right to vote in presidential and municipal elections. In February, Ohio gave women the right to vote in presidential elections. In March, Arkansas gave women the right to vote in the primaries. In April, Michigan, Nebraska, and Rhode Island all granted women presidential suffrage. These were victories indeed, but there was still a great deal of work to be done.

Led by Catt, the members of NAWSA persisted in their efforts until finally, in 1918, Congress began to show support for woman suffrage. On February 10, the House of Representatives passed the suffrage amendment by one vote. The next day, without a moment wasted, the suffragists began to pressure their senators to vote their approval. To their frustration, the Senate vote was delayed several months. During the long wait, Catt and the other NAWSA leaders wrote letters and circulated petitions intended to keep the issue of woman suffrage in front of the senators.

Finally the Senate announced that it would vote on the suffrage amendment on September 26. Catt wrote in a letter to President Wilson: "We hope that you who have proved yourself a miracle worker on many occasions may be able to produce another wonder on Monday—the wonder of putting vision where there was none before."[62]

Another delay pushed the vote back to October 1. The tally was sixty-two in favor, thirty-four against—just two votes short of the two-thirds majority needed to pass the amendment. One last push lay ahead.

Victory at Last

The 1918 election placed many supporters of woman suffrage in Congress, greatly increasing chances of the amendment's passage during the next congressional session. In the meantime, Catt was at work on something that had been her dream for a long time. She created an organization called the League of Women Voters to educate women on parliamentary procedure and government practices.

When Congress met for its sixty-sixth session, on May 19, 1919, Catt stayed at home, not wanting to witness another disappointment. But this time, when the lawmakers voted on the suffrage amendment, the dream finally became reality. The House of Representatives voted in favor of woman suffrage, 304 to 89. The Senate vote revealed 56 in favor, 25 against. The suffragists had won. Now it was up to the individual states to ratify.

The Chicago Daily News *reports that Tennessee ratified the Nineteenth Amendment, allowing women the right to vote.*

Catt, who found out about the victory over the phone, danced with joy when she heard the news. After reveling in the long-overdue success, she immediately sent telegrams to the state governors, encouraging them to ratify as soon as possible. Within four months, the suffragists had ratification by seventeen of the necessary thirty-six states. They were almost halfway to victory. But by fall, there had been little further progress. So Catt, never willing to give up a fight, packed her bags and headed west on a "Wake up America" tour.

Catt met with legislators, governors, women suffragists, and

Sixtp-sixth Congress of the United States of America;

At the First Session,

Begun and held at the City of Washington on Monday, the nineteenth day of May, one thousand nine hundred and nineteen.

JOINT RESOLUTION

Proposing an amendment to the Constitution extending the right of suffrage to women.

Resolved by the Senate and House of Representatives of the United States of America in Congress assembled (two-thirds of each House concurring therein), That the following article is proposed as an amendment to the Constitution, which shall be valid to all intents and purposes as part of the Constitution when ratified by the legislatures of three-fourths of the several States.

"ARTICLE ————.

"The right of citizens of the United States to vote shall not be denied or abridged by the United States or by any State on account of sex.

"Congress shall have power to enforce this article by appropriate legislation."

F. H. Gillett

Speaker of the House of Representatives.

Thos. R. Marshall

Vice President of the United States and President of the Senate.

A facsimile of the Nineteenth Amendment, brought before the sixty-sixth Congress of the U.S. and ratified by a majority vote in 1920.

anyone else who would listen to her, urging the states to call special sessions in order to vote for ratification of the Suffrage Amendment. Catt was convincing and inspiring. In November and December, five more states ratified and in January 1919, eight more followed suit.

By spring, the war had ended and four more states ratified the amendment, making thirty-five states total. Only one more was needed to win. Catt headed for Nashville, Tennessee, to offer support to the suffragists there who were desperately trying to persuade their legislators to ratify. Finally, in the smoldering afternoon heat on August 18, the Tennessee representatives voted. The vote was tied at 48 to 48 when suddenly a young representative from a small mountain county changed his vote because his mother, a suffragist herself, had made him promise his support. This last-minute switch won final victory for woman suffrage. Finally, after seventy-two years of hard work, struggle, and sacrifice, American women could vote.

Catt and the other suffragists were elated. Most of them had devoted years of work to the cause. For Catt, it had been a lifetime. Those brave women who had started them on the road to victory weren't even alive to see them win. But Catt's work was not finished. She continued to advocate women's rights and remained especially active in her international work until her death in 1947. Her organization, the League of Women Voters, is still influential today.

NOTES

Chapter 1: Votes for Women

1. Quoted in Aileen S. Kraditor, *The Ideas of the Woman Suffrage Movement*. New York: W. W. Norton, 1981, p. 18.

2. Quoted in Kraditor, *The Ideas of the Woman Suffrage Movement*, p. 20.

3. Alan Brinkley, *The Unfinished Nation: A Concise History of the American People, Volume Two, From 1865*. New York: McGraw-Hill, 1993, p. 576.

4. Marjorie Spruill Wheeler, *One Woman, One Vote: Rediscovering the Woman's Suffrage Movement*. Troutdale, OR: Newsage Press, 1995, p. 11.

Chapter 2: Elizabeth Cady Stanton (1815–1902): Torchbearer for Women

5. Quoted in Alma Lutz, *Created Equal: A Biography of Elizabeth Cady Stanton, 1815–1920*. New York: John Day, 1940, p. 4.

6. Elizabeth Cady Stanton, *Eighty Years and More: Reminiscences 1815–1897*. Boston: Northeastern University Press, 1993, p. 20.

7. Quoted in Lutz, *Created Equal*, p. 35.

8. Quoted in Winifred E. Wise, *Rebel in Petticoats: The Life of Elizabeth Cady Stanton*. New York: Chilton, 1960, p. 146.

9. Quoted in Wise, *Rebel in Petticoats*, p. 153.

10. Quoted in Lutz, *Created Equal*, p. 90.

11. Quoted in Lutz, *Created Equal*, p. 132.

12. Quoted in Lutz, *Created Equal*, p. 137.

13. Quoted in Lutz, *Created Equal*, p. 204.

14. Stanton, *Eighty Years and More*, pp. 467–68.

Chapter 3: Susan B. Anthony (1820–1906): "Failure Is Impossible"

15. Quoted in Rheta Childe Dorr, *Susan B. Anthony: The Woman Who Changed the Mind of a Nation*. New York: Frederick A. Stokes, 1928, pp. 12–13.

16. Quoted in Katherine Anthony, *Susan B. Anthony: Her Personal History and Her Era*. New York: Doubleday, 1954, p. 102.

17. Quoted in Anthony, *Susan B. Anthony*, p. 102.

18. Quoted in Alma Lutz, *Susan B. Anthony*. Boston: Beacon Hill Press, 1960, p. 38.

19. Quoted in Lutz, *Susan B. Anthony*, p. 94.

20. Quoted in Dorr, *Susan B. Anthony*, p. 201.

21. Quoted in Lutz, *Susan B. Anthony,* p. 200.

22. Quoted in Lutz, *Susan B. Anthony*, p. 291.

23. Quoted in Lutz, *Susan B. Anthony*, p. 310.

Chapter 4: Lucy Stone (1818–1893): Voice of the Women

24. Quoted in Alice Stone Blackwell, *Lucy Stone: Pioneer Woman Suffragist*. Boston: Little, Brown, 1930, p. 74.

25. Quoted in Elinor Rice Hays, *Morning Star: A Biography of Lucy Stone, 1818–1893*. New York: Harcourt, Brace & World, 1961, p. 64.

26. Quoted in Hays, *Morning Star*, p. 70.

27. Quoted in Blackwell, *Lucy Stone*, p. 90.

28. Quoted in Andrea Moore Kerr, *Lucy Stone: Speaking Out for Equality*. New Brunswick, NJ: Rutgers University Press, 1992, p. 106.

29. Quoted in Hays, *Morning Star*, p. 131.

30. Quoted in Hays, *Morning Star*, p. 153.

31. Quoted in Blackwell, *Lucy Stone*, p. 201.

32. Quoted in Hays, *Morning Star*, p. 183.

33. Quoted in Hays, *Morning Star*, p. 240.

34. Quoted in Blackwell, *Lucy Stone*, p. 243.

35. Quoted in Blackwell, *Lucy Stone*, p. 305.

Chapter 5: Anna Howard Shaw (1847–1919): A Woman Pioneer

36. Quoted in Anna Howard Shaw, *The Story of a Pioneer*. New York: Harper & Brothers, 1915, p. 56.

37. Quoted in Shaw, *The Story of a Pioneer*, p. 110.

38. Quoted in Shaw, *The Story of a Pioneer*, p. 151.

39. Shaw, *The Story of a Pioneer*, p. 151.

40. Quoted in Shaw, *The Story of a Pioneer*, p. 182.

41. Shaw, *The Story of a Pioneer*, p. 232.

42. Shaw, *The Story of a Pioneer*, p. 301.

43. Quoted in Helen Christine Bennett, *Women in Civic Work*. New York: Dodd, Mead and Company, 1915, p. 252.

44. Quoted in National American Woman Suffrage Association, Pamphlet from Anna Howard Shaw's memorial service, 1938.

Chapter 6: Alice Paul (1885–1977): A Militant Leader

45. Quoted in Inez Hayes Irwin, *The Story of Alice Paul and the National Woman's Party*. Fairfax, VA: Denlinger's Publishers, 1977, p. 7.

46. Quoted in Irwin, *The Story of Alice Paul*, p. 30.

47. Quoted in Midge Mackenzie, *Shoulder to Shoulder*. New York: Knopf, 1975, p. 134.

48. Quoted in Linda G. Ford, *Iron-Jawed Angels: The Suffrage Militancy of the National Woman's Party 1912–1920*. Lanham, MD: University Press of America, 1991, p. 55.

49. Quoted in Ford, *Iron-Jawed Angels*, p. 45.

50. Quoted in Ford, *Iron-Jawed Angels*, p. 91.

51. Quoted in Irwin, *The Story of Alice Paul*, p. 402.

52. Quoted in Irwin, *The Story of Alice Paul*, pp. 420–21.

53. Wheeler, *One Woman, One Vote*, p. 293.

54. Maud Younger, "Revelations of a Woman Lobbyist," *McCall's*, September/October/November 1919, p. 58.

55. Quoted in Ford, *Iron-Jawed Angels*, p. 256.

Chapter 7: Carrie Chapman Catt (1859–1947): "The Winning Plan"

56. Quoted in Jacqueline Van Voris, *Carrie Chapman Catt: A Public Life*. New York: Feminist Press, 1987, p. 5.

57. Quoted in Van Voris, *Carrie Chapman Catt*, p. 6.

58. Quoted in Van Voris, *Carrie Chapman Catt*, p. 12.

59. Carrie Chapman Catt and Nettie Rogers Shuler, *Woman Suffrage and Politics*. Seattle: University of Washington Press, 1969, p. 20.

60. Quoted in Van Voris, *Carrie Chapman Catt*, p. 83.

61. Quoted in Van Voris, *Carrie Chapman Catt*, p. 140.

62. Quoted in Mary Grey Peck, *Carrie Chapman Catt: A Biography*. New York: Octagon Books, 1975, p. 98.

1815
Elizabeth Cady Stanton is born in Johnstown, New York.

1818
Lucy Stone is born in West Brookfield, Massachusetts.

1820
Susan B. Anthony is born in Adams, Massachusetts.

1847
Anna Howard Shaw is born in Newcastle-on-Tyne, England.

1848
Elizabeth Cady Stanton makes a demand for woman suffrage at the first women's rights convention in Seneca Falls, New York.

1851
Susan B. Anthony and Elizabeth Cady Stanton begin to work closely together for women's rights.

1855
Elizabeth Cady Stanton appears before the New York State legislature on behalf of the Married Woman's Property Law.

1859
Carrie Chapman Catt is born in Ripon, Wisconsin.

1861
Civil War begins.

1863
Elizabeth Cady Stanton and Susan B. Anthony organize the Women's National Loyal League to educate women about political issues surrounding the war; the league generates a petition demanding the abolition of slavery by a constitutional amendment.

1868
The Fourteenth Amendment to the U.S. Constitution, guaranteeing citizenship for black men, is adopted.

1869
Two suffrage associations emerge: the National Woman Suffrage Association (NWSA), headed by Elizabeth Cady Stanton and Susan B. Anthony, and the American Woman Suffrage Association (AWSA), led by Lucy Stone and Henry Blackwell; women gain suffrage in the Wyoming Territory.

1870
The Fifteenth Amendment to the Constitution, guaranteeing black men the vote, is adopted; the *Woman's Journal,* a suffrage paper, is published by Lucy Stone and Henry Blackwell.

1872
Susan B. Anthony votes illegally in Rochester, New York.

1885
Alice Paul is born in Moorestown, New Jersey.

1890
The two American suffrage associations unite to form the National American Woman Suffrage Association (NAWSA); Wyoming joins the union and becomes the first state to grant women suffrage.

1893
Lucy Stone dies.

1902
Elizabeth Cady Stanton dies.

1906
Susan B. Anthony dies.

1912
Alice Paul founds the Congressional Union.

1913
Alice Paul organizes a suffrage parade in Washington, D.C., on the eve of Woodrow Wilson's inauguration.

1917
Alice Paul's National Woman's Party pickets the White House; many are arrested and jailed; those jailed go on hunger strikes and are force-fed.

1919
The Nineteenth Amendment to the U.S. Constitution, granting women the vote, is approved by Congress and sent to the states for ratification; Anna Howard Shaw dies.

1920
The Nineteenth Amendment to the U.S. Constitution is adopted and the women of the United States are allowed to vote.

FOR FURTHER READING

Ruth Ashby and Deborah Gore Ohrn, *Herstory: Women Who Changed the World*. New York: Viking, 1995. An interesting collection of 120 short biographies of notable women from ancient Egypt to the twentieth century. It is organized chronologically with cross-indexes and photos.

Florence Horn Bryan, *Susan B. Anthony: Champion of Women's Rights*. New York: Julian Messner, 1947. This story of the life of Susan B. Anthony is an intriguing history of one of America's most influential historical figures. Written specifically for younger readers, it provides an intimate look at her life and career.

Ellen Carol Dubois and Gerda Lerner, *The Elizabeth Cady Stanton–Susan B. Anthony Reader: Correspondence, Writing, Speeches*. Boston: Northeastern University Press, 1992. Readers get a firsthand look into the partnership and friendship of Elizabeth Stanton and Susan Anthony as expressed in their own words through their letters, speeches, and writings.

Eleanor Flexner, *Century of Struggle*. Cambridge, MA: Harvard University Press, 1975. An inspiring book about the grass-roots women's movement in the United States, including the suffrage struggle, women's education, labor, and property rights.

Eileen Heckart et al., eds., *Great American Women's Speeches*. A collection of some of the most moving and effective speeches given by American women throughout history.

William Jay Jacobs, *Great Lives: Human Rights*. New York: Simon & Schuster, 1990. A collection of minibiographies of historical figures who fought for human rights, including several leaders of the women's rights and woman suffrage movements.

Martha Solomon, ed., *A Voice of Their Own: The Woman Suffrage Press, 1840–1910*. Tuscaloosa: University of Alabama Press, 1991. This 233-page book includes chapters with sample writings by various authors from eight suffrage presses, the *Lily*, the *Una*, the *Revolution*, the *Woman's Journal*, the *Woman's Tribune*, the *Woman's Column*, the *Farmer's Wife*, and the *Woman's Exponent*.

WORKS CONSULTED

Katherine Anthony, *Susan B. Anthony: Her Personal History and Her Era*. New York: Doubleday, 1954. A thorough biography of Anthony, including details of both her public and private life.

Helen Christine Bennett, *Women in Civic Work*. New York: Dodd, Mead, 1915. Sketches of more than ten different suffragists which have been published serially in the *Pictorial Review* and the *American Magazine*.

Alice Stone Blackwell, *Lucy Stone: Pioneer Woman Suffragist*. Boston: Little, Brown, 1930. A biography of Lucy Stone, thoughtfully written by her daughter. It offers an intimate look at Lucy Stone's life from childhood to death.

Harriot Stanton Blatch and Theodore Stanton, *Elizabeth Cady Stanton as Revealed in Her Letters, Diary, and Reminiscences*. New York: Harper & Brothers, 1922. A collection of Stanton's thoughts and reminiscences as they appear in her personal letters and journals, narrated and edited by her daughter.

Alan Brinkley, *The Unfinished Nation, A Concise History of the American People, Volume Two: From 1865*. New York: McGraw-Hill, 1993. A concise account of American history from Reconstruction through modern times.

Mari Jo and Paul Buhle, *The Concise History of Woman Suffrage*. Chicago: University of Illinois Press, 1978. A brief record of the woman suffrage movement from grass-roots to the introduction of the Suffrage Amendment in 1920.

Carrie Chapman Catt and Nettie Rogers Shuler, *Woman Suffrage and Politics*. Seattle: University of Washington Press, 1969. The story of the suffrage movement as recorded by Carrie Chapman Catt, two-time president of the National American Woman's Suffrage Association.

Rheta Childe Dorr, *Susan B. Anthony: The Woman Who Changed the Mind of a Nation*. New York: Frederick A. Stokes, 1928. This book looks at Anthony in her role as women's rights leader and political organizer.

Ellen Dubois and Karen Kearns, *Votes for Women: A 75th Anniversary Album*. San Marino: Huntington Library, 1995. A chronological look at the woman suffrage movement as illustrated by the collections at the Huntington Library.

G. Thomas Edwards, *Sowing Good Seeds*. Portland: Oregon Historical Society Press, 1990. This book covers Susan B. Anthony's journeys to Oregon in 1871, 1896, and 1905 to support the suffrage movement. The book includes newspaper accounts to show how she worked the media, raised support, and spread the news about woman suffrage. Includes historic photographs.

Elizabeth Glendower Evans and Carol A. Rehfisch, "The Woman's Party—Right or Wrong?" *New Republic*, September 26, 1923. This article debates the leading issues of the Woman's Party during 1923, shortly after women gained suffrage.

Margaret Finnegan, *Selling Suffrage: Consumer Culture and Votes for Women (Popular Cultures, Everyday Lives)*. New York: Columbia University Press, 1999. A study of the woman suffrage movement through the changes in American public life. It provides a good look at how political culture was shaped by commercial culture in the decades around 1900.

Linda G. Ford, *Iron-Jawed Angels: The Suffrage Militancy of the National Woman's Party 1912–1920*. Lanham, MD: University Press of America, 1991. This book chronicles the events of the National Woman's Party, lead by Alice Paul, and examines its effects on the final ratification of the Nineteenth Amendment.

Elizabeth Griffith, *In Her Own Right: The Life of Elizabeth Cady Stanton*. New York: Oxford University Press, 1984. Focuses on the personal story of Stanton from childhood to women's rights leader. It offers an intimate look into the complexities of her dynamic personality.

Florence Howe Hall, *Julia Ward Howe and the Woman Suffrage Movement*. New York: Arno & The New York Times, 1969. A collection of writings and lectures composed by Julie Ward Howe, a poet, patriot, philosopher, and key player in the women's rights movement during her lifetime.

Elinor Rice Hays, *Morning Star: A Biography of Lucy Stone, 1818–1893*. New York: Harcourt, Brace & World, 1961. The life of Lucy Stone from her childhood to her death. This book covers her many contributions to the women's rights movement, especially regarding woman suffrage, and her dedication to the fight for human rights for all Americans.

Inez Hayes Irwin, *The Story of Alice Paul and the National Woman's Party*. Fairfax, VA: Denlinger's Publishers, 1977. A biographical account of the life of militant suffragist Alice Paul, which also provides a record of the Woman's Party and the activities of its leaders.

Johanna Johnston, *Mrs. Satan*. New York: G.P. Putnam's Sons, 1967. The story of Victoria Claflin Woodhull and her sister Tennessee Claflin, two wealthy women conducting lives of unbelievable freedom during the late 1800s. At a time when most women were struggling against oppressive social conventions, these two sisters were ignoring society and living as they pleased.

Andrea Moore Kerr, *Lucy Stone: Speaking Out for Equality*. New Brunswick, NJ: Rutgers University Press, 1992. This book considers many of Stone's accomplishments and struggles, with an emphasis on her public life.

Aileen S. Kraditor, *The Ideas of the Woman Suffrage Movement*. New York: W. W. Norton, 1981. An overview of the ideas employed by woman suffrage supporters and their opposition. This book also provides information on society's perceptions and beliefs about the role of women during the struggle for woman suffrage.

Trevor Lloyd, *Suffragettes International*. New York: American Heritage Press, 1971. A concise, yet informative, overview of the worldwide campaign for women's rights.

Linda J. Lumsden, *Rampant Woman: Suffragists and the Right of Assembly*. Knoxville: University of Tennessee Press, 1997. A book on the relationship between women and freedom of expression, covering topics such as the right of association, open-air campaigns, petitions, and picketing in the context of the history of women's rights.

Alma Lutz, *Created Equal: A Biography of Elizabeth Cady Stanton, 1815–1920*. New York: John Day, 1940. An authoritative biography of Stanton, founder of the women's rights movement. This book gives a detailed account of her life and provides a bounty of historical information about the women's rights and woman suffrage causes.

——, *Susan B. Anthony*. Boston: Beacon Hill Press, 1960. A biography of Anthony providing a look into her early years, her lifelong career as a leader in the women's rights movement, and her influence on later generations.

Midge Mackenzie, *Shoulder to Shoulder*. New York: Knopf, 1975. A documentary history of the militant suffragettes in Britain.

The National American Woman Suffrage Association, *Victory, How Women Won It: A Centennial Symposium 1840–1940*. New York: H. W. Wilson Company, 1940. A book that describes and honors the women and events that made up the woman suffrage movement.

National American Woman Suffrage Association, pamphlet from Anna Howard Shaw's memorial service, 1938. This pamphlet contains several eulogies by unidentified authors.

Mary Grey Peck, *Carrie Chapman Catt: A Biography*. New York: Octagon Books, 1975. A comprehensive biography of the life of

Carrie Chapman Catt, including her service to women internationally after woman suffrage was achieved.

Sheila Rowbotham, *A Century of Women.* New York: Penguin Books USA, 1997. A comprehensive look at the achievements and events of women in the United States and in Britain throughout the nineteenth century.

Anna Howard Shaw, *The Story of a Pioneer.* New York: Harper & Brothers, 1915. An autobiography of Shaw, covering her life from her earliest memories to her work with the woman suffrage movement.

Lynn Sherr, *Failure Is Impossible: Susan B. Anthony in Her Own Words.* New York: Random House, 1995. A collection of Anthony's speeches, letters, and quotes organized by theme and linked by the author's biographical commentary.

Elizabeth Cady Stanton, *Eighty Years and More: Reminiscences 1815–1897.* Boston: Northeastern University Press, 1993. An autobiography including a significant amount of family history and spanning Stanton's life nearly to its end. Although it is written to cover her entire life story, it focuses primarily on her career as a women's rights leader.

Doris Stevens and Carol O'Hare, *Jailed for Freedom.* Troutdale, OR: Newsage Press, 1995. A dramatic documentation of women's struggle to win the vote through militant actions. The author reveals, among other facts, the imprisonment, vilification, and brutality women experienced during their fight for their eventual political victory.

Rosalyn Terborg-Penn, *African American Women in the Struggle for the Vote, 1850–1920.* Bloomington: Indiana University Press, 1998. A comprehensive portrait of the African American women who fought for the right to vote. The author analyzes the women's own stories of why they joined and how they participated in the American woman suffrage movement. It provides an interesting look at the differences between the black and white woman suffrage struggles.

Jacqueline Van Voris, *Carrie Chapman Catt: A Public Life.* New York: Feminist Press, 1987. The story of Carrie Chapman Catt's life, highlighting her public achievements as a women's rights and woman suffrage leader.

Doris Weatherford, *A History of the American Suffragist Movement.* Santa Barbara: ABC-CLIO, 1998. This book chronicles the long and torturous campaign to secure woman suffrage. It emphasizes the connections of the women's movement to the other great nineteenth-century reform movements of abolitionism and temperance.

Marjorie Spruill Wheeler, *One Woman, One Vote: Rediscovering the Woman's Suffrage Movement*. Troutdale, OR: Newsage Press, 1995. A collection of speeches, lectures, and writings of various leaders in the woman's suffrage movement. This anthology is a companion piece to the television special "One Woman, One Vote," produced by the Educational Film Center, for the PBS "American Experience" series.

Winifred E. Wise, *Rebel in Petticoats: The Life of Elizabeth Cady Stanton*. New York: Chilton, 1960. A biographical account focusing on Stanton's career as a pioneer feminist.

Maud Younger, "Revelations of a Woman Lobbyist," *McCall's*, September/October/November 1919. A member of the Woman's Party recalls her personal experience as a suffrage activist.

Daughters of Temperance, 35, 36
Declaration of Sentiments, 25–26
Dennett, Mary Ware, 73
divorce, women's right to, 11, 13
Douglass, Frederick, 12, 13, 26, 35

Equal Rights Amendment (ERA), 83

Fifteenth Amendment, 17, 41
Floyd Country Advocate, 86–87
Foster, Ellen, 85
Fourteenth Amendment, 16–17, 31, 54–55

Garrison, William Lloyd, 12, 49
Grant, Ulysses S., 84
Greeley, Horace, 84

Higginson, Thomas Wentworth, 17
House of Representatives, U.S.
  passage of Suffrage Amendment by, 93, 94
Howe, Julia Ward, 17

Idaho, 19, 89
International Council of Women, 44, 45, 89
International Woman Suffrage Alliance (IWSA), 90

Kansas, 19

League of Women Voters, 95
Lily (newspaper), 27
Lincoln, Abraham, 29
Livermore, Mary, 17, 55

Mallon, Winifred, 74
Married Women's Property Bill, 40
May, Samuel, 51
Michigan, 93
Mississippi Valley Conference (1892), 87
Mitchell, Maria, 85
Mott, James, 25
Mott, Lucretia, 11, 12–13, 23, 24, 35

National American Woman Suffrage Association (NAWSA), 9, 32
  Shaw, as head of, 66–67
  Southern strategy of, 19–20
National Woman's Party (NWP), 20
  founding of, 77–78
  protest at Metropolitan Opera, 80–81
National Woman Suffrage Association (NWSA), 17, 31, 32, 41, 55, 73
  disagreement with Congressional Union, 77
  disagreement with National Woman's Party, 78
  formation of, 44
  weaknesses of, 88

PICTURE CREDITS

Cover photos: Archive Photos
American Stock/Archive Photos, 15
AP, 30
Archive Photos, 9, 12, 28, 34, 36, 37, 38, 52, 55, 67, 75, 77
Bettmann/Corbis, 16, 26, 50, 88
Corbis, 44, 51, 57, 59, 68, 89, 92
Hulton-Deutsch Collection/Corbis, 69, 79
Illustrated London News/Archive Photos, 90
Library of Congress, 10, 11, 18, 23, 24, 33, 42, 43, 45, 47, 48
Minnesota Historical Society/Corbis, 65
Museum of the City of N.Y./Archive Photos, 85
Popperfoto/Archive Photos, 27
Stock Montage Inc., 14, 21, 25, 64, 71, 72, 73, 81, 82, 93, 94, 95
Underwood & Underwood/Corbis, 62

ABOUT THE AUTHOR

Kristina Dumbeck lives in Solana Beach, California, with her husband, Jason, and daughter, Sadie. She is a graduate of La Sierra University, where she studied English literature and writing. She has written for software companies, public relations departments, and health-care organizations. She has also worked as a teacher and tutor of students in grades K–12, and has worked closely with students of English as a Second Language programs.